Teacher's Notes

Black and White pages 13–16

Before listening: Worksheet p. 13, task 1

- Copy and hand out the worksheet. Explain that each speech bubble contains one verse of the song.
- Ask pupils to separate the words and rewrite the texts a)–e) on the given lines.

While listening: Worksheet p. 13, task 2

- Play the song. Ask pupils to write down the order of the verses in the given spaces. Explain that some verses are repeated.
- Play the song again. Check the answers with the whole class and sing the song.
  Key: 1b-2c-3a-4d-5e-6a-7e-8a

While listening: Worksheet p. 14, tasks 3, 4

- Pupils listen to the song again and write down the words in the song that rhyme with the words on the worksheet. They then add more words to their lists.
  Key: white, write, sight, night, light ... and also bite, fight, kite, might...
  understand, land ... and also hand, sand...
  see, liberty, ... and also be, key, me...
- Collect the words on the board or a transparency.
- Encourage pupils to write poems using the rhyming words and to illustrate their work. If necessary, do an example with the class first: e.g. *A cat is black / A cat is white / It catches mice by day and night...*

After listening: Two e-mail projects pages 15–16

Project 1:
- Ask pupils to read the e-mail messages on p. 15. Help them with difficult words: Jill: *Empire State Building* building in New York with 102 stories; George: *a pain* someone irritating; Ben: *Yorkshire Dales* valleys in the county of Yorkshire (north-east England)
- Pupils decide whose e-mail they would like to answer and give reasons for their choice.
- Pupils write short e-mails to one e-pal.
- Contact the website below, preferably with the class, for more up-to-date requests for e-pals:
  http://www.kids-space.org
- Encourage pupils to make and keep up e-mail contact.

Project 2:
- Ask pupils to write e-mail requests for e-pals.
- Send the requests to 'Kidslink' at:
  http://www.geocities.com/EnchantedForest/7065/
- ➜ Ask parents in advance to allow pupils to use their computer at home.

BLACK AND WHITE (Three Dog Night)

1. The ink is black/The page is white/Together we learn to read and write/A child is black/A child is white/The whole world looks upon the sight/A beautiful sight

2. now a child can understand/That this is the law of land/All the land

CHORUS: The world is black/The world is white/It turns by day and then by night/A child is black/A child is white/Together they grow to see the light/To see the light

4. And now at last we plainly see/We'll have a dance of liberty/Liberty

5. The world is black/The world is white/It turns by day and then by night/A child is black/A child is white/The whole world looks upon the sight, a beautiful sight

The chorus followed by Verse 5 followed by the chorus.

Come on ... Get it! Get it! Oh yeah! Yeah!/Keep it up now around the world/ Little boys and little girls ... Yeah!

Lyrics: David Arkin; Music: Earl Robinson; © Templeton Publ. Co. Inc. for D, A, CH: Essex Musikvertrieb GmbH, Hamburg.

Colours p. 17

Before listening: Worksheet p. 17, task 1

- The pupils write down as many colours and associations as possible on a piece of paper.

While listening: Worksheet p. 17, task 2

- Ask pupils to read the lines in task 2. Difficult words: *mellow* (here) a warm feeling; *rarely* seldom; *sparkling* that shines when the sun is on it. Play the song. Pupils put the lines into the correct order.
- Check the answers with the whole class.
  Key: 2, 4, 1, 5, 3

After listening: Worksheet p. 17, tasks 3, 4

- Write one verse on the board to show the structure of the verses: *a is the colour of b in the c when I rise...*
- With a partner, pupils decide on three colours and write new verses using the pattern. Pupils read out their verses and decide on the best ones. (You could sing these verses with the class.)
- Pupils can play this variation on the game "I spy" in a small group (also possible as a class activity or competition). In Britain, children play this game with letters instead of colours ("I spy with my little eye something beginning with 'd'.") The class could try this version, too.

COLOURS (Donovan)

Yellow is the colour of my true love's hair/In the mornin' when we rise,/In the mornin' when we rise,/That's the time, that's the time/I love the best.

Blue's the colour of the sky/In the mornin' when we rise,/In the mornin' when we rise,/That's the time, that's the time/I love the best.

Green's the colour of the sparklin' corn/In the mornin' when we rise,/In the mornin' when we rise,/That's the time, that's the time/I love the best.

Mellow is the feeling that I get/When I see her, um hmm./When I see her, uh huh./That's the time, that's the time/I love the best.

Freedom is a word I rarely use/Without thinkin', hmm hmm/Without thinkin', mm hmm/Of the time, of the time/When I've been loved.

Lyrics and Music: Donovan Leitch; © 1965 by Southern Music Publ. Co. Ltd., London for D: 1999 by Peermusic (Germany) GmbH Hamburg.

The Calendar Song   pages 18–19

Before listening: Worksheet p. 18, task 1

- Tell pupils that they are going to hear an easy song called "The Calendar Song" and the text of the song has twelve words only. Ask them to think about the title and guess what the twelve words are.
- Ask pupils to write their ideas on the worksheet.

While listening: Worksheet p. 18, tasks 1, 2

- Play the song. Pupils listen and tick off any words from their list in task 1 that they hear.
- Play the song again. Pupils write the months into the boxes. They then write the answers on the board.
  Key: 31 days = January, March, May, July, August, October, December; 30 days: April, June, September, November; 28 or 29 days: February

After listening: Worksheets pages 18–19, task 3

- Pupils work in groups of at least six and have enough worksheets for a whole calendar. They add the days, dates and name of the month to each frame. They can draw pictures to go with each month. (Alternative: pupils make collages using photos from magazines.)
- Display the calendars in the classroom.
- Pupils can practise pronouncing the names of the months and then sing "The Calendar Song".

CALENDAR SONG (Boney M)

January, February, March, April, May, June, July (2)
August, September, October, November, December (2)

(Both parts are repeated a number of times.)

Don't Worry Be Happy   p. 20

Before listening

- Ask pupils: "What things make you happy/sad/worried?"

While listening: Worksheet p. 20, task 1

- Hand out the worksheet. Pupils read out the words in the boxes. Check pupils' pronunciation.
- With a partner, pupils read the text and try to fill in the words correctly. Play the song so that pupils can check their answers.
  Difficult words: *landlord* a man who rents you a room; *rent* the money you give to a landlord every month; *to litigate* to take someone to court; *cash* money; *to frown* to look angry; *to pass* to go away
- Check the answers with the whole class.
  Key: *wrote, double, bed, late, smile, down*
- Play the song a second time. Ask pupils to join in.

After listening: Worksheet p. 21, tasks 2, 3

- Hand out p. 21. Pupils work in pairs. They write down the information they get from their partner about Mr. Smiley's week. This is good practice for the past tense.
- Pupils work in pairs. They take turns to ask their partner questions about his/her week. Pupils can use similar questions to those in task 2. Pupils record the answers in the diary.

Further suggestions:
- First ask pupils to think of words and phrases:
  – to say that they are worried or unhappy,
  – to cheer someone up.
  Pupils write a dialogue between two friends: one of them is worried and unhappy about something, the other tries to cheer her/him up.

DON'T WORRY, BE HAPPY (Bobby McFerrin)

Here's a little song I wrote/You might want to sing it note for note/Don't worry, be happy/In every life we have some trouble/But when you worry you make it double/Don't worry, be happy/Don't worry, be happy now (ooh)/Don't worry, be happy/Don't worry, be happy/Don't worry, be happy

Ain't got no place to lay your head/Somebody came and took your bed/Don't worry, be happy/The landlord say your rent is late/He may have to litigate/Don't worry, be happy/(Look at me I'm happy) (ooh)/Don't worry, be happy/I give you my phone number/When you're worried call me/I'll make you happy/Don't worry, be happy

Ain't got no cash, ain't got no style/Ain't got no girl to make you smile/But don't worry, be happy/'cause when you're worried/Your face will frown/And that will bring everybody down,/So, don't worry, be happy/Don't worry, be happy now (Ooh)/Don't worry, be happy/Don't worry, be happy/Don't worry, be happy/Don't worry, be happy/Don't worry, don't worry, don't do it, be happy/Put a smile on your face/Don't bring everybody down like this/Don't worry, it will soon pass/Whatever it is, don't worry, be happy...

Lyrics and Music: Bobby McFerrin; © by BMG Music Publishing International, for D, A, CH: Musik-Edition Discoton GmbH, (BMG UFA Musikverlage), Munich.

El Condor Pasa pages 22-23

El Condor Pasa means "the condor is flying past".

Before listening

- Write the difficult construction from the song and an example on the board.
  If I could (be a film star), I surely would.
- Ask pupils to think of similar sentences, e.g.
  If I could do any job, I would be a ….;
  If I could live anywhere, I would live …

While listening: Worksheet p. 22, task 1

- Hand out the worksheet. Pupils read the text. Explain any new words / difficult lines (e.g. *swan* white bird that swims on lakes; *gives its saddest sound* it makes a very unhappy sound; *beneath* under). Pupils listen to the song and circle the mistakes.
- Play the song again. Pupils correct the mistakes. They can refer to the box at the bottom of the page. Pupils check their answers in pairs and then with the class.
  Key: sparrow/snail; hammer/nail; sail away; man/ ground; world; forest/street; earth/feet

After listening: Worksheet p. 23, tasks 2, 3

- In groups of 4–5, pupils find out the likes and dislikes of group members.
- Each group reports back to the class about what they have found out. (Tip: Put an example on the board to help less fluent students, e.g. *Chris would rather be Michael Jackson than Elton John and he'd rather be a tiger or a tree than a mouse or a football. Finally he'd rather be at sea now than in New York.*)
- Mini project: Ask pupils to make their own "I'd rather be …" poster with short texts and illustrations.
- Task 3 is suitable for better students or as homework.
  Idea: Collect and copy the texts to make a class reader, so that everyone has a chance to read all of the texts.

EL CONDOR PASA (Simon and Garfunkel)

I'd rather be a sparrow than a snail./Yes I would./If I could, I surely would. (Hmm)

I'd rather be a hammer than a nail./Yes I would./If I only could, I surely would. (Hmm)

Away, I'd rather sail away/Like a swan that's here and gone./A man gets tied up to the ground./He gives the world its saddest sound,/Its saddest sound. (Hmm)

I'd rather be a forest than a street./Yes I would./If I could, I surely would.

I'd rather feel the earth beneath my feet./Yes I would./If I only could, I surely would.

Lyrics and Music: Daniel A. Robles/Jorge Milchberg; © 1933/1963/1970 by Edward B. Marks Music Co., for D: Musikverlag Intersong GmbH, Hamburg

Our House pages 24-25

Before listening

- Write the song title on the board. Ask pupils to guess what the song is about. Write key words on the board.

While listening: Worksheet p. 24, task 1

- Play the song. Pupils check which of their ideas about the song were right.
- Play the song again. With a partner, pupils identify the missing lines. Check the missing text with the class.
  Key: The kids are playing up downstairs, He can't hang around, And it's usually quite loud, Nothing ever slows her down, Father gets up late for work, Then she sends the kids to school, Such a happy time
- Ask the pupils to find sentences in the song that tell them about the people in "Our House".

After listening: Worksheet p. 25, task 2

- Check that pupils understand the words at the bottom of p. 25. Pupils do the crossword puzzle in pairs.
  Key:

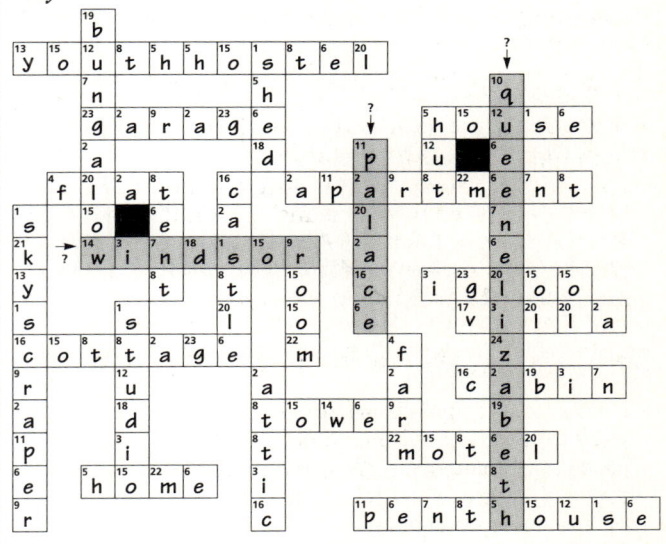

(crossword puzzle with answers: youth hostel, garage, flat, apartment, windsor, house, igloo, villa, cottage, cabin, tower, motel, home, penthouse)

- Copy the worksheet onto a transparency to check the answers.

After listening: Worksheet p. 26, tasks 3, 4

- Pupils can work in pairs on task 3 and individually on task 4.
Note: Present the pupils' work on wall charts. The class could have a rap competition to decide on the best rap.

OUR HOUSE (Madness)

Father wears his Sunday best/Mother's tired she needs a rest/The kids are playing up downstairs/Sister's sighing in her sleep (Ahh)/Brother's got a date to keep/He can't hang around/

Our house, in the middle of our street/Our house, in the middle of our …

Our house, it has a crowd/There's always something happening/And it's usually quite loud/Our mum she's so house-proud/Nothing ever slows her down/And a mess is not allowed

Our house, in the middle of our street/Our house, in the middle of our …/Our house, in the middle of our street/Our house, in the middle of our …/Something tells you that you've got to get away from it

Father gets up late for work/Mother has to iron his shirt/Then she sends the kids to school/Sees them off with a small kiss/She's the one they're going to miss/In lots of ways

Our house, in the middle of our street/Our house, in the middle of our …

I remember way back then when everything was true and when we would have such a very good time such a fine time/Such a happy time/And I remember how we'd play simply waste the day away/Then we'd say nothing would come between us two dreamers

Father wears his Sunday best/Mother's tired she needs a rest/The kids are playing up downstairs/Sister's sighing in her sleep/Brother's got a date to keep/He can't hang around

Our house, in the middle of our street/Our house, in the middle of our street/Our house, in the middle of our street/Our house, in the middle of our …

Our house, was our castle and our keep/Our house, in the middle of our street/Our house, that was where we used to sleep/Our house, in the middle of our street …

Lyrics: Cathal Smyth; Music: Christopher Foreman/Cathal Smyth; © 1982 EMI Music Publishing Ltd. London. Reproduced by permission of IMP Ltd.

Jeans On pages 27–28

Before listening: Worksheet p. 27, task 1 a)

- Ask pupils to unscramble the mixed-up words in task 1. Check their answers as a class.
  Key: *jeans, guitar, sunny, tiger, close, place, weekend, boring, dollar, morning, alright, pocket*

While listening: Worksheet p. 27, tasks 1 b), 2

- Play the song. Pupils tick the appropriate boxes.
  Key: *morning, alright, weekend, close, pocket, tiger, place*
- Play the song again. Pupils fill in the gaps in task 2. Check the answers with the whole class.
- Play the song again. Encourage pupils to sing along.

After listening: Worksheet p. 28, tasks 3, 4

- Pupils solve the *'clothes puzzle'*. Copy p. 28 onto a transparency to check the answers (see above).
- Pupils do the tandem exercise in task 4 in pairs.

- Show the class a transparency with the names of items of clothing for a short time. Ask pupils to write down as many of the items as they can remember.

JEANS ON (Dave Dundas)

When I wake up/In the morning light/I pull on my jeans/And I feel alright/I pull my blue jeans on/I pull my old blue jeans on/(I pull my blue jeans on/I pull my old blue jeans on: 3)

It's the weekend/And I know that you're free/So pull on your jeans/And come on out with me/(I need to have you near me/I need to feel you close to me: 2)

You and me/We'll go motorbike-riding/In the sun and the wind and the rain/I got money in my pocket/Got a tiger in my tank/And I'm King of the Road again

I meet ya in the usual place/I don't need a thing/Such a pretty face/And I need to have you near me/I need to feel you close to me/(I need to have you near me/I need to feel you close to me: 2)

You and me/We'll go motorbike-riding/In the sun and the wind and the rain/I got money in my pocket/A tiger in my tank/And I'm King of the Road again

When I wake up/In the morning light/I pull on my jeans/And I feel alright/(I pull my blue jeans on/I pull my old blue jeans on: 3) … (last stanza: 3)

Lyrics and Music: Dave Dundas/Greenaway; © by Air Music London Ltd., for D, A, CH: EMI Music Publishing Gemany GmbH, Hamburg.

June Afternoon pages 29–30

Before listening

- Pupils compare a June afternoon to a January afternoon. Write key words in two columns on the board.

While listening: Worksheet p. 29, task 1

- Hand out p. 29. Each line of the song contains an extra word. Play the song. Pupils follow the text.

- Pupils underline the extra words and write them on the lines. In b) pupils make a phrase with the first letter of the extra words. Check the answers in class.
  Key: *always, happy, old, then, silly, usually, now, new, yes, and, free, terrible, easy, right, never, only, our, not, in, nearly, hello, yellow, dirty, evening, poor, all, red, Kate – A HOT SUNNY AFTERNOON IN HYDE PARK*

After listening: Worksheet p. 30, tasks 1, 2, 3

- In pairs, pupils find words in the song that they associate with a 'park'. They can also add their own ideas. Collect ideas on the board or a transparency.
- Ask pupils to describe what they see in the picture to the class or a partner.
- In pairs, pupils write dialogues and read them out.

After listening: Worksheet p. 30, task 4

- Explain what a diamond poem is, e.g.
  January
  cold, snowy
  skating, skiing, riding on a sleigh
  happy, excited
  January
- Pupils can use a dictionary if they need to. They can illustrate their poems, too.
- Display the results in class.

JUNE AFTERNOON (Roxette)

Didn't I tell you everything is possible in this déjà vu?/Try the river boat, the carousel, feed the pigeons, barbecue/Look at all the people, happy faces all around./Smiling, throwing kisses, busy making lazy sounds

It's a bright June afternoon,/it never gets dark. Wah-wah!/Here comes the sun./Get your green green tambourine,/Let's play in the park. (Wah-wah!)/Here comes the sun

Some folks are on blankets, slowly daydreaming/and reaching for their food./Let's go buy an ice-cream and a magazine with an attitude/and put on a cassette, we can pretend that you're a star/'cause life's so very simple/just like la-la-la

It's a bright June afternoon,/it never gets dark. Wah-wah!/Here comes the sun./Get your green green tambourine,/let's play in the park. (Wah-wah!)/Here comes the sun, comes the sun

There's a painter painting his masterpiece./There are some squirrels jumping in the trees./There's a wide-eyed boy with a red balloon./All my life I've longed for this afternoon.

It's a bright June afternoon/it never gets dark. Wah-wah!/Here comes the sun./Get your green green tambourine/Let's play in the park. Wah-wah!/Here comes the sun

It's a bright June afternoon/Let's play in the park. Wah-wah!/Here comes the sun

Get your green green tambourine/It never gets dark. Wah-wah!/Here comes the sun/It never gets dark/(Let's play in the park:2)/Here comes the sun

Lyrics/Music: Per Gessle; © Jimmy Fun Music, Örebro, Sweden.

Lemon Tree pages 31–35

Before listening: Worksheet p. 31, task 1

- Hand out p. 31. Pupils read the text and fill in the words. They can check their answers with a partner.

While listening: Worksheet p. 31, task 1

- Play the song twice. Pupils can check their answers and correct any mistakes.
  Key: *room, afternoon, do, waiting, car, like, yesterday, see, head, sitting, go, bed, good, want, toy*
- Check the answers with the class and sing the song.

After listening: Worksheets pages 32–33, task 2

- After preparing the materials pupils play the games in tasks 2 (pages 32–33) and 3 (pages 33–35).

After listening

- Pupils find phrases that express how the singer feels (bored, isolated…) and why he is unhappy (it's raining, he's wasting time…). Collect phrases on the board.
- Talk about the meaning of the song and especially the lemon tree. (See DER FREMDSPRACHLICHE UNTERRICHT, Heft 34, pages 12–14.)

LEMON TREE (Fool's Garden, 1995)

I'm sitting here in a boring room/It's just another rainy Sunday afternoon/I'm wasting my time/I got nothing to do/I'm hanging around/I'm waiting for you/But nothing ever happens – and I wonder

I'm driving around in my car/I'm driving too fast, I'm driving too far/I'd like to change my point of view/I feel so lonely, I'm waiting for you/But nothing ever happens – and I wonder

CHORUS: I wonder how, I wonder why/Yesterday you told me 'bout the blue blue sky/and all that I can see is just a yellow lemon tree/I'm turning my head up and down/I'm turning turning turning turning turning around/And all that I can see is just another lemon tree Sing da, da ... dee, da...

I'm sitting here, I miss the power/I'd like to go out taking a shower/But there's a heavy cloud inside my head/I feel so tired, put myself into bed/Where nothing ever happens – and I wonder

Isolation is not good for me/Isolation, I don't want to sit on a lemon tree/I'm stepping around in a desert of joy/Maybe anyhow I'll get another toy/And everything will happen/And you wonder

I wonder how/I wonder why/Yesterday you told me 'bout the blue blue sky/and all that I can see is just another lemon tree/I'm turning my head up and down/I'm turning turning turning turning turning around/(And all that I can see: 3)/Is just a yellow lemon tree

And I wonder, wonder/I wonder how, I wonder why/yesterday you told me 'bout the blue blue sky/(And all that I can see:3)/Is just a yellow lemon tree.

Lyrics/Music: Volker Hinkel/Peter Freudenthaler; © 1995 by EMI MMC Musikverlag GmbH & Co. KG, Hamburg.

I Can't Help Myself p. 36

Before listening

- Write the song title on the board and explain that: "I can't help myself" = *I can't stop myself doing … even though I shouldn't*. Ask pupils to think of situations where people cannot help themselves.

While listening: Worksheet p. 36, task 1

- Hand out the worksheet and ask pupils to tick the verbs they hear as they listen to the song. They can compare their answers with a partner's.
- Play the song again. Ask pupils to complete their lists. Check the answers with the whole class.
  Key: be, change, come, help, hold, kiss, love, say, stop, talk, tell, think, turn, wait, want

After listening: Worksheet p. 36, task 2

- In small groups/with a partner, pupils write a verse giving the singer's ex-girlfriend's side of the story.
- Pupils can read out or display their texts in class.
- Pupils enjoy singing this song very much, so they could sing along to the CD.

**I CAN'T HELP MYSELF
(I LOVE YOU, I WANT YOU)** (Kelly Family)

If I would tell you/how much you mean to me/I think you wouldn't understand it/So I wait, I wait/until this day comes/When you will understand me

But I can't help myself/I can't stop myself/I am going crazy/And I can't stop myself,/Cannot control myself,/I'm going crazy

CHORUS: And I love you,/I want you/I wanna talk to you,/I wanna be with you/And I love you,/I want you/I wanna talk to you,/I wanna be with you

I cannot change it,/I'm sure not making it/One big hell of a fuss/I cannot turn my back/I've got to face the fact/Life without you is hazy

CHORUS: …

Kiss me, thrill me,/don't say goodbye/Hold me, love me,/don't say goodbye/Ooooooh, don't say goodbye/But I can't help myself,/And I can't stop myself,/I am going crazy/I cannot turn my back/I've got to face the fact/Life without you is hazy

CHORUS: …/Oh uho uho oh, kiss me goodbye

Lyrics/Music: The Kelly Family; © KEL-Life Music Production GmbH, Köln.

Respect Yourself pages 37–38

Before listening: Worksheet p. 37, task 1a)

- Ask pupils to look at the words in the bubble. Explain any new words, e.g.
  resignation when someone does not try to make a situation better and just gives up
  isolation when someone feels all alone
  fair play when someone acts fairly towards others
  destiny what will happen to someone
- Pupils connect the words that rhyme by drawing lines between them.
  Key: know, rainbow; game, aim; mind, blind; way, pray; resignation, isolation; inside, hide; destiny, free

While listening: Worksheet p. 37, task 1b)

- Pupils use the rhyming words to fill in the gaps. They can check their answers in pairs.
- Play the song again. Check the answers (see key above).

After listening: Worksheet p. 38, tasks 2, 3

- For task 2 pupils shut their eyes and concentrate on the singer's voice and the music.
- Each pupil puts the things that came to mind while he/she was listening into the mind map.
- In task 3, encourage pupils to experiment with language, write their own poems and add drawings.
- Display the finished texts in class.
  ➜ Allow pupils to do more than one task if they wish.

RESPECT YOURSELF (DJ Bobo)

Respect yourself/Respect yourself/Don't run away/Respect yourself/Respect yourself/Come on help each other out/And respect yourself

You don't know, no, what you don't know/I like the colors of the rainbow/Respect is the name of the game/Respect yourself and you never miss your aim/If you show weakness/You gotta let them know/You don't know, no, what you don't know/If you wanna grow, say no, just go

CHORUS: Respect yourself/Change your mind/Respect yourself/Don't be blind/Respect yourself/And you will see the light/Respect yourself/And you will find your way/So practise what you pray/Don't run away/Respect yourself/(Respect yourself: 2)/ You will see the light

Don't care about what people say/Believe in yourself and go your own way/Respect no resignation/Leave the *path of isolation/Don't care about what people say/ R.E.S.P.E.C.T. will never get away/Today, we stay, and pay attention anyway/Fair play every day don't run away*

Change your mind/Don't be blind/And you will see the light/And you will find your way/So practice what you pray/Don't run away/Respect yourself/Change your mind/Respect yourself/Don't be blind/Respect yourself/ And you will see the light/Respect yourself/And you will find your way/So practise what you pray/Don't run away/Respect yourself

If you're feeling weak so deep inside/No place to run no place to hide/R.E.S.P.E.C.T./Respect your destiny/If you don't know what is right or wrong/If you feel confused and your thoughts are gone/R.E.S.P.E.C.T./Respect yourself be free

(Respect yourself: 2)/So practise what you pray/(You will see the light: 2)

Respect yourself/Change your mind/Respect yourself/ Don't be blind/Respect yourself/And you will see the light/Respect yourself/And you will find your way/So practise what you pray/Don't run away/Respect yourself

(Respect yourself: 6)/You will see the light/(Respect yourself: 4)/Don't run away/Respect yourself

Lyrics/Music: R. Baumann/A. Breitung; © Edition Capricorn – EAMS Musikverlag, Bishop Songs Musikverlag.

The World In Perfect State pages 39-42

Before listening

- Pupils imagine that they are going on a trip to the North Sea. Ask them to say what they expect to see there. Collect ideas on the board or a transparency.

While listening: Worksheet p. 39, task 1

- Hand out the worksheet. Ask pupils to cut out the text fragments.
- Pupils listen to the song, reconstruct the text and check the order of the text fragments with a partner.
- Play the song again. Check the answers with the class.

After listening: Worksheet p. 40, tasks 2, 3

- Present the homepage, Brucie and his friends. Don't forget to bring a map to show where New Zealand is!
- Talk about the aims of "Kids Caring For The Environment". Think of ways to achieve these aims.
- Collect ideas for a letter to Brucie. The pupils draft an e-mail in groups. Then they decide which e-mail to send to Brucie.

After listening: Worksheet p. 40, task 4

- Pupils do the tandem exercise first and then reconstruct the picture story.
- Pupils write a story to go with the pictures and stories in which Brucie and his friends try to stop pollution.

Teaching tip: This website is updated regularly. You will find stories, an online game, letters, pictures and a lot of information. Visit Brucie's homepage with the class.
http://www.brucecgull.com

THE WORLD IN PERFECT STATE (Hessel)

Garbage, beaches, dirty water/Filthy skies and no excuse for what we did/It's the work we have/Now the world is tired/Carry our dirt day after day/Year after year, why it's the bad way/Yeah, it's the bad way

CHORUS: I like to see the world in perfect state/Like you to meet me on a place that's great/I like to live on a place that's nice and cosy/I like to see the world in perfect state/ Why there's a good way/Yeah, that's the good way

The water's blue, blue and green/The sand so white you've never seen/The sky so clean/It's too long ago/ That we had the feeling/How it's real, now it's the dirt/ That really hurts/Oh it's the bad way/yeah, it's the bad way

CHORUS: …/Why there's a good way/Yeah, that's the good way

No one in the world can help me more/To make the sand so white/The water shines bright/And the sky is right/ What it's supposed to be/A place that's great to be/A clean beach baby, for you and me/Yeah, that's the right way

CHORUS: 2/(...)/Why that's a good way/Yeah, that's the good way/(...)/(That's the good way: 2)

Lyrics and Music: Ray McCannon; © Groene Weide Muziek BV, Terschelling Hoorn.

Simon Says pages 43–44

Before listening

- Write 'the body' on the board. Ask pupils to write any words which come to mind on the board. They then copy the mind map into their exercise-books.

While listening: Worksheet p. 43, task 1 a)

- Pupils listen to the song and tick any words in their mind map that they hear.
- Hand out p. 43. Play the song. In pairs or individually, pupils put the verses in the correct order. Play the song a third time, if necessary. Check the order with the class.
  Key: BACKBONE
- Pupils read the text and practise the actions.
- Encourage the class to sing along and do the actions.

After listening: Worksheet p. 43, tasks 1b), c)

- In small groups or pairs, pupils underline the actions in the song. They then think of six more actions and write them in the lines given.

- The class can play "Simple Simon". One pupil calls out actions, e.g. *Simple Simon says: Jump up and down.* If he/she calls out an action without saying *Simple Simon says...* the players do nothing. Those who do, are out. The last player left is the winner.

After listening: Worksheet p. 44, task 2

- Hand out p. 44. Pupils work in pairs. Copy the worksheet onto a transparency to check the answers. Explain any new words. **Key:**

↓F	↓H	A	N	D				M	
A	E	F→	I	↓N	G	E	R		R
C	A			↓L	O			↓E	↑A
E	D		E		S		L		
	↓K		G				E	B	
		N	M→	O	U	T	H		O	↓T
		R	E		T	O	O	F←	W	O
		A		E						E
		↑E	Y	E		K	C	E	N←	

- Pupils draw and label a picture of a person using the words they found in the puzzle.

SIMPLE SIMON SAYS (1910 Fruitgum Co.)

I'd like to play a game that is so much fun/And it's not so very hard to do/The name of the game is Simple Simon Says/And I would like for you to play it, too.

Put your hands in the air – Simple Simon says/Shake them all about – Simple Simon says/Do it when Simon says – And you will never be out.

Simple Simon says – Put your hands on your hips/Let your backbone slip – Simon says/Simple Simon says – Put your hands on your hips/Let your backbone slip – Simon says

Put your hands on your head – Simple Simon says/Bring them down by your side – Simple Simon says/Shake them to your left – Simple Simon says/Now shake them to your right (2)

Now that you have learned to play this game with me/You can see it's not so hard to do/Let's try it once again, this time more carefully/And I hope the winner will be you

Clap your hands in the air – Simple Simon says/Do it double time – Simple Simon says/Slow it down like before – Simple Simon says/Are you looking fine? – Simple Simon says

Now clap them high in the air – Simple Simon says/Do it double time – Simple Simon says...

Lyrics and Music: Elliot Chiprut; © 1967 by Kaskat Music Inc. for D, Musikverlag Intersong GmbH, Hamburg.

Top Of The World pages 45–48

Before listening

- Ask pupils to think of different jobs. Write the words on the board. Pupils copy down the list.

While listening: Worksheet p. 45, task 1

- Pupils listen to the song. They tick any jobs which are on the "before listening" list.
- Hand out p. 45. Play the song again. Pupils fill in the gaps. Ask them to add new words to their list of jobs.
  Key: *taxi driver, postal worker, office cleaner, ballet dancer, pop singer, ex-miner, single mother, bus driver, print worker, footballer*

After listening: Worksheet p. 46, tasks 2, 3

- Pupils do exercises 2 and 3 alone or in pairs.
- Copy the worksheet onto a transparency to check the answers. Pupils can start new word lists for *sports* by putting the sports into categories (summer/winter/team/indoor/outdoor/Olympic/… sports).
  Task 2: American football, ice hockey, table tennis, downhill skiing, horse-riding, windsurfing, high jump, basketball, roller-skating, weightlifting
  Task 3:

B→	A	S	K	E	T	B	A	L	L	↓H
	↓C		G	↓T				G	O	
	R		N	E				N	C	
D→	I	V	I	N	G			I	K	
Y	C		L	N				M	E	
B	K	S	C	I	T	S	A	N	M	Y
G	E	Y	S	N	O	T	N	I	M	D	A	B←
U	T	↑C						W		G→	O	L	F
↑R			G	N	I	K	↑S				
				R	E	C	C	O	S←		
		O	D	U	J	S←	A	I	L	I	N	G

After listening: Worksheet pages 46–48, task 4

- Pupils can play "Memory" in small groups. They will probably already know the rules. To save time in class, pupils can glue cardboard onto the back of the picture and word cards, and cut them out at home.
- Make sure that the pupils say the words for the sports when they turn the cards.

TOP OF THE WORLD (OLÉ, OLÉ, OLÉ) (Chumbawamba)

1. *Words on a postcard from far away/Spoke of a time long ago/Laughed ourselves daft on that Saturday/Singing "Here We Go"…*

2. *I'm a taxi driver/I'm a postal worker/I'm an office cleaner/I'm a striking docker/I'm a ballet dancer/I'm a zapatista/I'm a pop singer/I'm a winner –/I'm a winner, baby/I'm a winner, baby*

CHORUS: *Olé, Olé, Olé/Top of the world/I'm on top of the world …/Olé, Olé, Olé/Top of the world/I'm on top of the world …*

3. I'm a bricklayer/I'm an ex-miner/I'm a single mother/I'm a bus driver/I'm a political prisoner/I'm a print worker/I'm a footballer/I'm a winner –/I'm a winner, baby/I'm a winner, baby/

CHORUS: …/(First verse and CHORUS are repeated)

Lyrics and Music: Armath/A. Nutter/J. Abbott/D. Hamer/P. Greco/L. Watts/N. Hunter/A. Whalley/D. Bruce/J. Deja; © 1998 by Hans Kusters Music N.V., for D, A, CH: EMI Music Publishing Germany GmbH, Hamburg/Richard Kaun Musikverlag KG, Munich.

What A Wonderful World pages 49–51

Before listening: Worksheet p. 49, task 1

- Ask pupils to draw a picture of what they imagine a wonderful world to be like.
- Working in pairs, pupils describe their pictures.

While listening: Worksheet p. 50, tasks 2, 3

- Play the song. Pupils write down the colours in the first verse in the order that they hear them. They can colour in the picture and compare theirs with a partner's.
  Key: green, red, blue, white
- Pupils listen to the song again. They tick the words in task 3 that they hear. Check the answers with the class.
  Key: babies, clouds, colours, day, faces, friends, hands, night, people, rainbow, roses, trees

After listening: Worksheet p. 50, task 4

- Hand out and read p. 49. Explain any difficult words, e.g. *blessed* = which we can enjoy; *sacred* = holy
- Pupils identify the adjectives in the text. They write the adjectives and the nouns they describe in the box and then check their answers with a partner.
  Key: wonderful – world, green – trees, red – roses, blue – skies, white – clouds, bright/blessed – day, dark/sacred – night

After listening: Worksheet p. 51, task 5

- Pupils write the pairs of adjectives on the lines. With a partner, they can add more pairs to their lists.
- Collect the answers and the extra pairs on the board.
  Key: bad – good, cold – hot, sad – happy, small – big, dirty – clean, short – long, boring – interesting, slow – fast, noisy – quiet, difficult – easy, old – new, expensive – cheap

After listening: Worksheet p. 51, tasks 6, 7, 8

- Pupils read the tasks and select one they want to do.
- Make a class reader with the finished texts.

WHAT A WONDERFUL WORLD (Louis Armstrong)

I see trees of green, red roses, too,/I see them bloom for me and you,/And I think to myself: What a wonderful world!/I see skies of blue and clouds of white,/The bright blessed day, the dark sacred night,/And I think to myself: What a wonderful world!

The colours of the rainbow, so pretty in the sky,/Are also on the faces of people goin' by./I see friends shakin' hands, sayin "How do you do?"/They're really sayin' "I love you."

I hear babies cry, I watch them grow,/They'll learn much more than I'll ever know,/And I think to myself: What a wonderful world!/And I think to myself: What a wonderful world!/Yeah, I think to myself, what a wonderful world/ Oh yeah …

Lyrics and Music: George D. Weiss/George Douglas; © by Abilene Music Corp./Herald Square Music Co., for D, A, CH: Melodie der Welt, J. Michel KG, Musikverlag, Frankfurt/Eldorado Musikverlag GmbH, Hamburg.

Words pages 52–54

Before listening: Worksheet p. 52, task 1

- Hand out the worksheet. In pairs, pupils read the text and try to guess where the lines fit into the text.
  Tip: Pupils should look at the end-rhymes for help.

While listening: Worksheet p. 53, task 2

- Pupils listen to the song and check their answers to task 1. Check the text with the whole class.
  Key: A smile can bring you near to me, Let's start a brand-new story, A single word I say, To take your heart away, I'm here if you should call to me, And words are all I have, It's only words
- Play the song again and encourage pupils to join in.

After listening: Worksheet p. 53, task 2

- Before starting the game pupils say what they have learned about the speaker from the song text.
- Pupils prepare the materials for the game.
- Play *Bingo* in groups or as a class.

WORDS (Boyzone)

Smile an everlasting smile/A smile can bring you near to me/Don't ever let me find you gone/'Cause that would bring a tear to me

This world has lost its glory/Let's start a brand-new story/Now my love/You think that I don't even mean/A single word I say/It's only words/And words are all I have/To take your heart away

Talk in everlasting words/And dedicate them all to me,/And I will give you all my life/I'm here if you should call to me/You think that I don't even mean/A single word word I say/It's only words/And words are all I have/To take your heart away

It's only words/And words are all I have/To take your heart away/Da da …

This world has lost its glory/Let's start a brand-new story/ Now my love/You think that I don't even mean/A single word word I say/It's only words/And words are all I have/ To take your heart away/(It's only words/And words are all I have/To take your heart away: 3)

Lyrics/Music: Maurice Gibb/Robin Gibb/Barry A. Gibb; © by Gibb Brothers Music Ltd. for D, A, CH: Music-Edition Discoton GmbH (BMG UFA Musikverlage), Munich.

Macarena Worksheet p. 55

Before dancing

- Pupils practise the actions. One pupil calls out the instructions to the rest of the class.
  Put your right arm out!
  Put your left arm out!
  Put your right hand on your left arm!
  Put your left hand on your right arm!
  Put your right hand on your head!
  Put your left hand on your head!
  Put your right hand on your behind!
  Put your left hand on your behind!
  Move to the left and right three times!
  Jump to the left! And put your right arm out…

While playing the song

- Pupils listen to the song. Ask them to think how the words and music go with the actions. (The actions are usually done during the chorus.)
- Play the song again. Either the teacher or one of the pupils gives the instructions and demonstrates the actions. The class joins in.

After listening: Worksheet p. 55

- Pupils can draw pictures showing the actions.
- In groups of four, pupils think of other actions to go with the music. They can write new instructions and draw pictures to help the class learn the new dance.
- Each group presents its dance. If you have a large classroom, you can have a *Macarena* competition.

MACARENA *(Bayside Boys mix)*

I am not trying to seduce you …/When I dance they call me Macarena/And the boys, they say que soy buena/ They all want me, they can't have me/So they all come and dance beside me/Move with me, chant with me/ And if you're good, I'll take you home with me.

(CHORUS: Dale a tu cuerpo alegria Macarena/Que tu cuerpo es pa' darle alegria y cosa buena/Dale a tu cuerpo alegria Macarena/Ehhhh, Macarena: 2)

Now don't you worry about my boyfriend/The boy whose name is Vitorino/I don't want him, couldn't stand him/He was no good, so I … ha, ha, ha, ha, ha/Now come on, what was I supposed to do?/He was out of town and his two friends were sooooooo fine.

(CHORUS: 2)/I am not trying to seduce you … Macarena/ CHORUS (2)

Come and find me my name is Macarena/(…)/Que ta buena, come join me, dance with me and all you fellas chant along with me

Spanish chorus (5)

Lyrics/music: Antonio Romero/Rafael Ruiz; © 1993 by Grupo Editorial Discorama S. L./Nuevas Ediciones S. A./Canciones Del Mundo S. A., for D, A, CH: Neue Welt Musikverlag GmbH, Munich.

YMCA pages 56–58

Before listening

- Write the letters *YMCA* on the board and explain what they stand for (Young Men's Christian Association = a youth and community organisation that offers sport and health activities, social and personal development programmes, training opportunities and opportunities to go on exchange programmes.

While listening: Worksheet p. 56, task 1

- Hand out the worksheet. In pairs, pupils try to guess the missing words. Explain any new words.
- Play the song and let pupils check their answers.
- Play the song again. Check the answers as a class.
  Key: down, unhappy, go, time, feel, me, thing, shelf, today, feel, shoes, street, way, down, shoes

Note: Pupils enjoy singing along and dancing to the music.

After listening: Worksheet p. 57, tasks 2, 3

- In pairs, pupils do tasks 2 and 3. Check the answers using a transparency.

↓F	E	E	↓L		↓S		→P	U	T
I			I		T			↓C	
N		→S	T	A	R	↓T		A	
D		T		Y		A		R	
→H	A	V	E			K	→B	E	
		→K	N	O	↓W		E		
↓C				A				↓S	
O		→H	A	N	→G		↓G	A	
→M	A	K	E		→T	E	N	J	O	Y
E			L		T				
		→P	I	C	K		→D	O	

- Pupils write about what they did the previous weekend – possibly as homework – using the verbs in task 3.

After listening: Worksheet p. 58, tasks 4, 5

- The class looks at the information in task 4 and pupils give their preference for particular activities.

- Project: In groups, pupils talk about youth groups in their town. They collect materials (brochures, posters, leaflets, photos) and write checklists and reports.
- Display the work in class.
➡ Find out more about **The YMCA in Britain** or **The YMCA in the USA** on the internet.

YMCA (The Village People)

Young man, there's no need to feel down/I said, young man, pick yourself off the ground/I said, young man, 'cause you're in a new town/There's no need to be unhappy.

Young man, there's a place you can go/I said, young man, when you're short on your dough/You can stay there, and I'm sure you will find/Many ways to have a good time.

CHORUS: It's fun to stay at the YMCA/It's fun to stay at the YMCA/They have everything for young men to enjoy./You can hang out with all the boys./It's fun to stay at the YMCA/It's fun to stay at the YMCA/You can get yourself clean/You can have a good meal/You can do whatever you feel.

Young man, are you listening to me/I said, young man, what do you want to be/I said, young man, you can make real your dreams/but you've got to know this one thing./No man does it all by himself/I said, young man, put your pride on the shelf/And just go there, to the YMCA/I'm sure they can help you today.

CHORUS: ...

Young man, I was once in your shoes,/I said, I was down and out with the blues/I felt, no man cared if I were alive / I felt the whole world was so jive/That's when someone came up to me/and said young man take a walk up the street/There's a place there called the YMCA/They can start you back on your way.

CHORUS: .../YMCA/And just go to the YMCA ...

Lyrics: V. Willis; Music: Jacques Morali; © 1978 for Scorpio Music, France, for D, A, CH: La Carte Music Verlags-GmbH, Hennef.

I Just Called To Say I Love You pp. 59–60

Before listening: Worksheet p. 59, task 1

- Pupils collect words related to "love" in a mind map. They compare their mind maps with a partner's. Collect the words on the board or on a transparency.

While listening: Worksheet p. 59, task 2

- Pupils read task 2 carefully before listening to the song. They tick the phrases that begin with the word 'no'. Check the answers with the class.
- Play the song again. Pupils put the lines into the correct order. Check the order with the class.

Key: No... 1. New Year's Day...; 2. chocolate-covered candy hearts; 3. first of spring; 4. song to sing; 5. April rain; 6. flowers bloom; 7. wedding day...; 8. summer's high; 9. warm July; 10. harvest moon...; 11. autumn breeze; 12. falling leaves; 13. Libra sun; 14. Halloween; 15. giving thanks...

After listening: Worksheet p. 60, tasks 3, 4

- Pupils do the wordsearch in pairs. They can write the words they find on the lines given in task 4. Check the answers in class.

		H	A	L	L	O	W	E	E	N		J	U	N	E
↓E				↓C					↓F						
A					H	S	A	T	U	R	D	↓A	Y	↓N	
S	Y	↓A	D	S	R	U	H	T	H	I		P		E	
T	L	U			I				C	D		R		W	
E	↓B	U	T	U	E	S	D	A	Y	R	A	I		Y	
R	A	↓J	U		T				A	Y		L		E	
Y	N	M			M	R	E	B	↑M	E	C	E	D	A	
A	K	N			A		O	C	T	O	B	E	R		
D	H	C	H	R	I	S	T	M	A	S	D	↓A	Y		S
G	O		↓S		E					U				D	
N	L		U		V	S	P	R	I	N	G			A	
I	I		N		E			J	A	N	U	A	R	Y	
X	D		D							S					
O	A		A		S	U	M	M	E	R	T				
↑B	Y	G	U	Y	F	A	W	K	E	S	N	I	G	H	T

After listening: Worksheet p. 61, tasks 5, 6

Note: Pupils can work in pairs on the task of their choice.

- Check that pupils understand the phrases in task 5a). They fill in the grid. Check the answers.
- Encourage pupils to write their own texts for task 5b) (short short story, a poem, a report, etc.) and draw pictures. Display the results in class.
- Explain what a haiku is. Pupils can create sequences of haikus, e.g. one for each day of the week, month or season.

I JUST CALLED TO SAY I LOVE YOU (Stevie Wonder)

No New Year's Day to celebrate,/No chocolate-covered candy hearts to give away,/No first of spring,/No song to sing,/In fact here's just another ordinary day.

No April rain,/No flowers bloom,/No wedding Saturday within the month of June,/But what it is, is something true,/Made up of these three words that I must say to you.

CHORUS: I just called to say I love you,/I just called to say how much I care,/I just called to say I love you,/And I mean it from the bottom of my heart.

No summer's high,/No warm July/No harvest moon to light one tender August night,/No autumn breeze,/No falling leaves,/Not even time for birds to fly to southern skies.

No Libra sun,/No Halloween,/No giving thanks to all the Christmas joy you bring,/But what it is, though old so new,/To fill your heart like no three words could ever do.

(CHORUS: ... 2)/Of my heart, baby of my heart ...

Lyrics and Music: Stevie Wonder; © by Jobete Music Co. Inc./Black Bull Music Co., USA, for D, A, CH: EMI Music Publishing Germany GmbH, Hamburg.

Christmas Time pages 62–64

Before listening

- Sing a Christmas carol with pupils (cf. *Happy Christmas*, Klett 3-12-586202). Then ask the class if they know any modern Christmas songs.

While listening: Text p. 62

- Copy the text onto a transparency.
- Play the song. Uncover the text line by line. Pupils focus on the words and music.

After listening: Worksheet p. 63, tasks 1, 2, 3

- Pupils read the text and solve the crossword. Check the answers with the whole class.
  Key task 1:

  (Crossword answers: 1 WINTER, 2 SNOWFLAKE, 3 LIGHTS, 4 KISS, 5 PRIDE, 6 HEART, 7 FAMILY, 8 SKY, 9 YEAR, 10 CHESTNUT, 11 FRIENDS)

- Pupils do tasks 2 and 3 alone or in pairs.
  Key task 2: candle, tree, cracker, Santa Claus, present, holly, star, chimney, turkey

After listening: Worksheet p. 64, task 4

- Read Carly's homepage with the pupils.
- Pupils design their own Christmas homepage.

Teaching tip: Around Christmas you can find numerous interesting sites on the internet, some of which are worth visiting especially with younger pupils. A good starting-point is the Welford and Wickham School, a small primary school:
http://www.wickham.newbury.sch.uk
You will also find Carly's homepage there.

Christmas Time *(Backstreet Boys)*

There is something special/About this time of year/A Christmas feeling's everywhere/I just got home to join you/I've been away too long/But now I'm back/To share my love/Friends are really like/One big family/Filled with love/To last throughout the year

CHORUS: Christmas time, time to share our love/Come and join the tidings to the world/Christmas time the best time of the year/Yes it's Christmas time/Christmas time ...

You and me together/Sleigh ride in the park/Loving kiss/Straight from the heart/Snowflakes falling to me and you/A smell of chestnuts in the air/And Christmas lights/They gleam across the sky/It's Christmas time

CHORUS: ...

Do you remember?/Everything felt so nice/When I held you close to me/Do you remember?/Those cold Christmas nights/When we saw the world in harmony

CHORUS: Christmas time, time to share our love/Come and join the tidings to the world (repeated)

Lyrics and Music: Veit Renn/Joe Smith/Johnny Wright; © by Zomba Enterprises Inc. for D, A, CH: Discoton GmbH, (BMG UFA Musikverlage), Munich.

Note: At the time of publication (April 2001) all internet addresses contained in this book were current.

Black and White by 3 Dog Night

1. The words of the song "Black and White" are given below but the spaces between the words are missing. Rewrite the text correctly from a)–e) in the lines below.

a) Theworldisblacktheworldiswhiteitturnsbydayandthenbynightachildisblackachildiswhitetogethertheygrowtoseethelighttoseethelight

b) Theinkisblackthepageiswhitetogetherwelearntoreadandwriteachildisblackachildiswhitethewholeworldlooksuponthesightabeautifulsight

c) Andnowachildcanunderstandthatthisisthelawofallthelandalltheland

d) Andnowatlastweplainlyseewe'llhaveadanceoflibertyliberty

e) theworldisblacktheworldiswhiteitturnsbydayandthenbynightachildisblackachildiswhitethewholeworldlooksuponthesightabeautifulsight

a) The world is black

b) The ink

c) And now a child

d) And now at last

e) The world is black

2. What is the correct order of the verses? Listen to the song and write the letters a)–e) in the spaces below. (Some of the verses are sung twice.)

1 _____ 2 _____ 3 _____ 4 _____ 5 _____ 6 _____ 7 _____ 8 _____

© Templeton Publ. Co. Inc. for D, A, CH: Essex Musikvertrieb, Hamburg

3. **Write down words from the song that rhyme with the words below. Then, add other words that rhyme to your lists.**

   white

   understand

   see

4. **Write a new verse for the song with some of the rhyming words you found in 3. (Tip: Think of other things that are black and white.) Draw a picture about your new verse in the box.**

   ## Black and White

Project 1: Making friends on the internet.
1. Read the following internet messages from six young people.
2. Say who you would like to have as an e-pal.
   EXAMPLE: *I'd like to have Gracie as an e-pal because she likes to go to the movies.*

Jill, Farmingdale, Long Island, USA
Hi! This is Jill talking to you. I live in Farmingdale, Long Island, which is near New York City! I've lived here for three years. I love New York! Have you ever been there? I've been up the Empire State Building 20 times! I go to New York most weekends and go shopping. New York has everything! I like to buy clothes and CDs and books. My other hobbies besides shopping are swimming, bike riding and travelling. My parents and I like to travel everywhere (well, almost). What's it like where you live? Please write and tell me! Maybe I'll come and visit! Until then, 'bye from the Big Apple.

George, Manchester, England
All my friends call me Boot, so you should too. It's short for football boot. They call me this because I play football all the time. I think football's brilliant. I started playing football when I was 6 years old. My favourite team of all is Manchester United. My sister thinks football is stupid, but that's because she's no good at it. Write to me if you want to talk about football or sisters who are a pain.

Carleen, Montreal, Canada
My name is Carleen, and I live in Montreal, Canada. I love to dance and to write stories. What I'd like most of all is to be a great singer one day. I sing every day for at least an hour. I sing along to the radio or a CD. My favorite singer is Celine Dion. I know the words to every one of her songs by heart. It's my dream to meet her one day. My parents promised me I can start singing lessons next year, and I'm so excited! So who are your favorite singers? What would you like to do when you are older? Please write and tell me!

Patrick, Seattle, Oregon, USA
Hello out there! I love all kinds of sports, as well as watching TV, playing computer games, surfing the net, and writing e-mails to people all over the world. So far I have 30 e-pals from six different countries. We talk about sports, our favorite computer games, websites, TV programs, and about a lot of other cool things. I've learned a lot about many interesting places from my e-pals. So what can you tell me about you and your country? I'm waiting!

Gracie, San Francisco, California, USA
Hi! My hobbies are going to rock concerts and the movies, reading and being with my friends! My favorite groups are the Backstreet Boys and Boyzone. They are so cool! My favorite movie of all time is "Titanic". It is so sad and romantic! I can't tell you what my favorite book is because I like too many! Besides books, the most important thing I own is my mobile phone. I take it everywhere so I can talk to my friends all the time. I also like meeting new friends on the internet, and I always write back to people who write to me. So write to me!

Ben, Yorkshire, England
My name is Ben. I come from a really big family and we live in a big house in the country. I have two sisters and three brothers. Sometimes we fight with each other, but usually we get on just fine. Our parents bought us a big dog named Spotty. We also have two cats (Higgins and Rawley) who just walked into our garden one day and stayed. My favourite thing to do is to rollerblade with my brothers and sisters. I also like skateboarding. I'd really like to hear what you like to do!

3. Now answer one of the e-mails in the screen below.

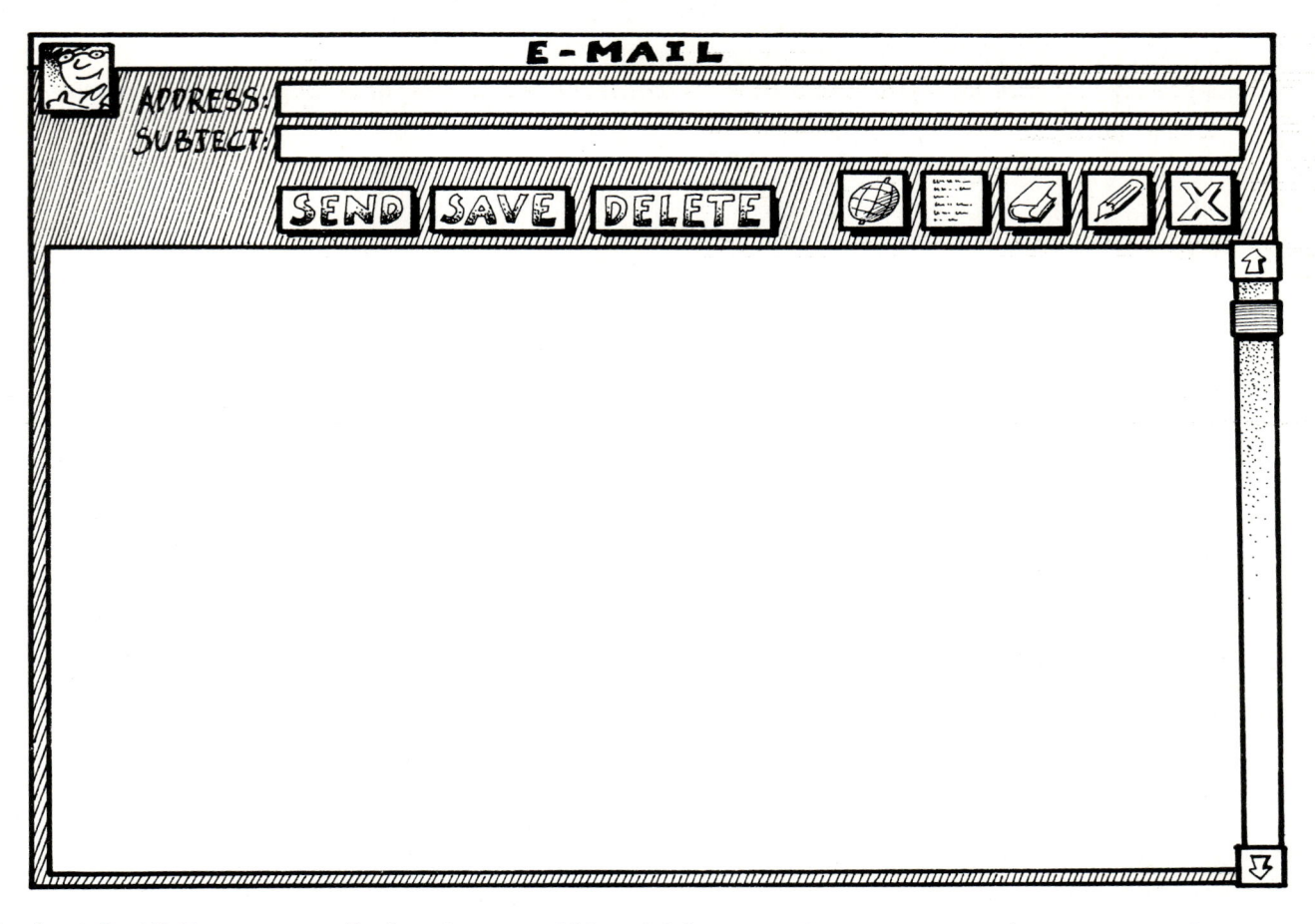

Project 2: Write an e-mail about yourself in which you ask someone to be your e-pal.

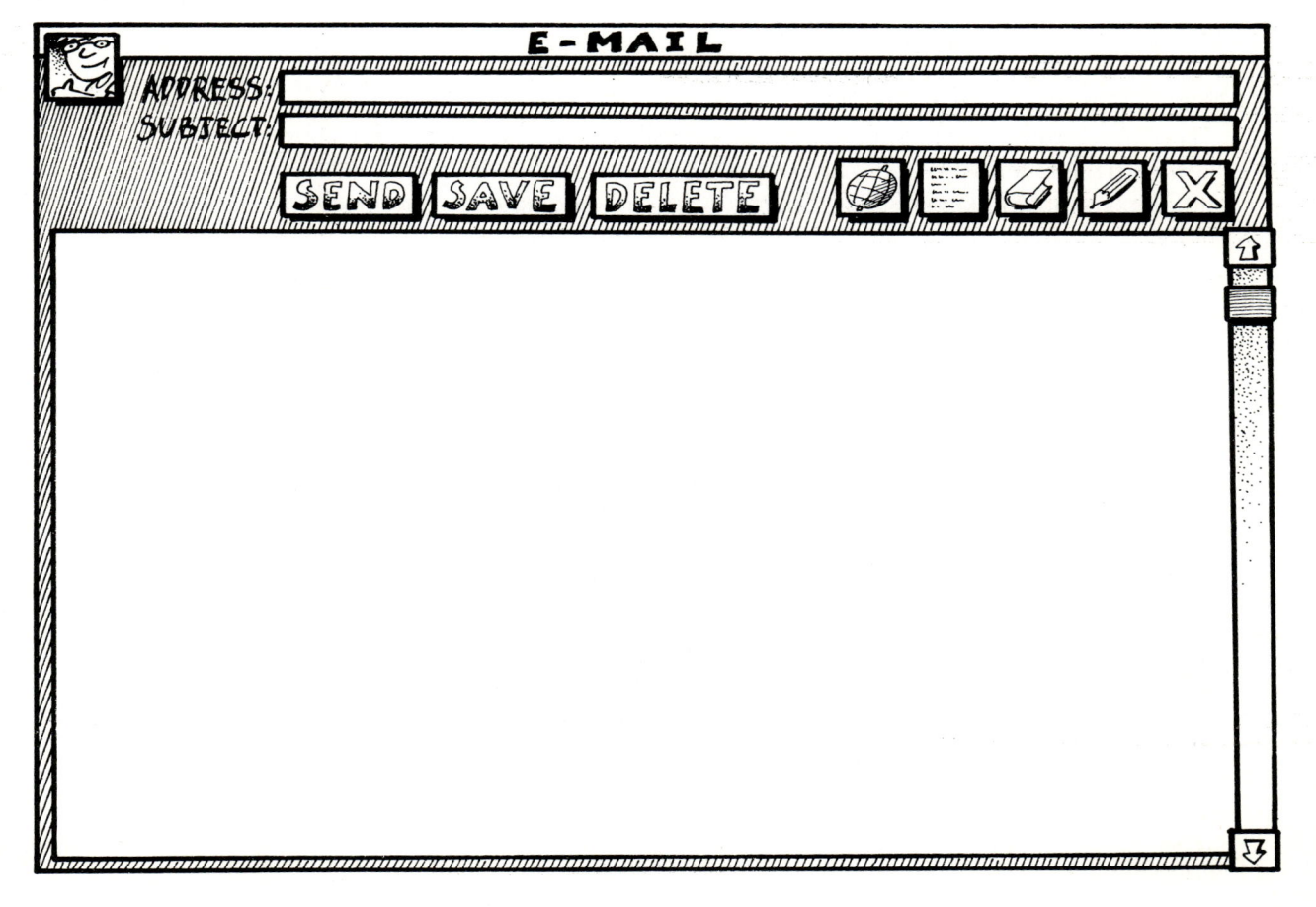

Colours by Donovan

1. **Collect all the colours you know in a mind map like the one below. Then write down the things you associate with these colours.**

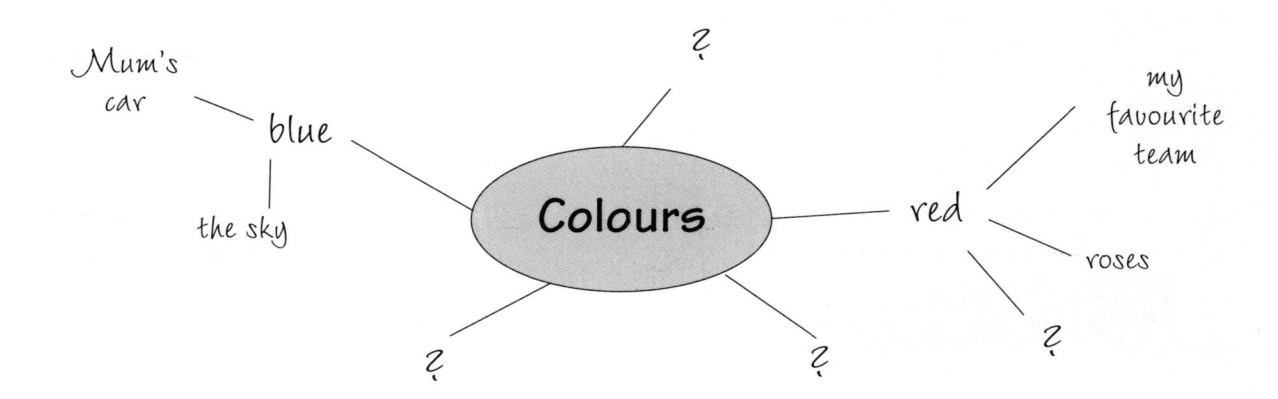

   Mind map:
   - Colours
     - blue — Mum's car, the sky
     - ?
     - red — my favourite team, roses
     - ?
     - ?
     - ?

2. **Read the sentences in the box and then listen to the song.**
   Put the sentences in the order (1–5) in which you hear them in the song.

Blue is the colour of the sky	
Mellow is the feeling that I get	
Yellow is the colour of my true love's hair	
Freedom is a word I rarely use	
Green's the colour of the sparklin' corn	

3. **Work with a partner. Think of three colours you both like. Then write new verses for the song.**

   _____
   _____
   _____
   _____
   _____
   _____

4. **Play "I spy" with your classmates.**
   You say "I spy with my little eye something that is (your colour choice), and your classmates guess what you are looking at.

The Calendar Song by Boney M.

1. The text of "The Calendar Song" is easy to understand because there are only twelve words in it. What do you think the words are? Write them down.

   _____

   _____

2. How many days does each month have? Write the months under the correct headings.

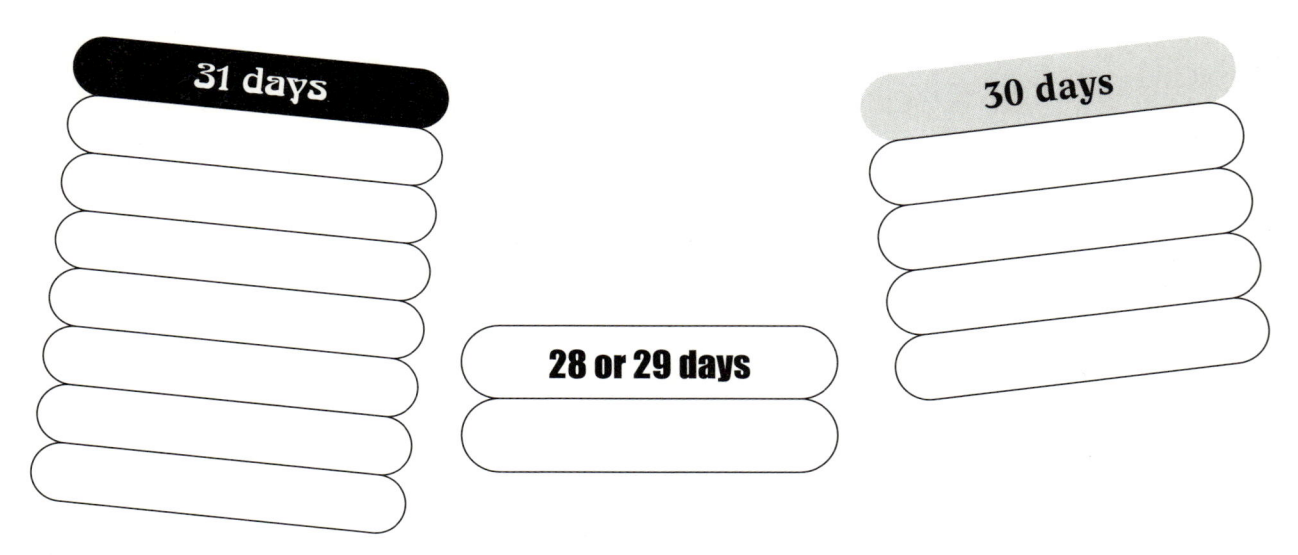

   31 days

   28 or 29 days

   30 days

3. Make a class calendar. For each month put in:
   - the name of the month,
   - the correct number of days in the month,
   - the days of the week,
   - a picture for the month.

   EXAMPLE

   SUN. = SUNDAY   MON. = MONDAY
   TUES. = TUESDAY   WED. = WEDNESDAY
   THUR. = THURSDAY FRI. = FRIDAY
   SAT. = SATURDAY

Don't Worry, Be Happy by Bobby McFerrin

1. Listen to the song and fill in the missing words. Be careful! You won't need all of them.

road • bed • down • bad • double • apple • cat • wrote • smile • stone • small • late

Here's a little song I _____
You might want to sing it note for note
Don't worry, be happy
In every life we have some trouble
But when you worry you make it _____
Don't worry, be happy
Don't worry, be happy now. Ooh ....
Don't worry, be happy ...

Ain't got no place to lay your head
Somebody came and took your _____
Don't worry, be happy
The landlord say your rent is _____
He may have to litigate

Don't worry, be happy
Look at me I'm happy. Oooh ...
Don't worry, be happy
I give you my phone number
When you're worried call me
I'll make you happy
Don't worry, be happy

Ain't got no cash, ain't got no style
Ain't got no girl to make you _____
But don't worry, be happy
'Cause when you're worried
Your face will frown
And that will bring everybody _____
So, don't worry, be happy
Don't worry, be happy now. Ooh ...
Don't worry, be happy ...
Don't worry, don't do it, be happy

Put a smile on your face
Don't bring everybody down like this
Don't worry, it will soon pass
Whatever it is, don't worry, be happy ...

© by BMG Music Publishing International,
for D, A, CH: Musik-Edition Discoton, Munich

2. Work with a partner. Partner A fills in one chart and Partner B fills in the other. Take turns asking and answering questions about Mr. Smiley's week. Write down what you learn about Mr. Smiley and draw a smiling face 😀 or a sad face ☹.

Was Mr. Smiley happy / worried on …?

Yes, he was. / No, he wasn't.

Why was Mr. Smiley happy / worried on …?

Because he …

Partner A

Day	Happy or worried	Mr. Smiley's week
Monday		
Tuesday	😀	a nice birthday present from his wife
Wednesday		
Thursday	😀	a funny film on TV in the evening
Friday	☹	to the doctor
Saturday		
Sunday		

Partner B

Day	Happy or worried	Mr. Smiley's week
Monday	😀	a new computer
Tuesday		
Wednesday	☹	strange noises in the house at night
Thursday		
Friday		
Saturday	☹	his key in the park
Sunday	😀	to the cinema with friends

3. Which things made your partner happy or worried last week? Ask him/her questions and fill in the diary below. You can draw a happy or a worried face in the boxes.

…'s week			
Monday		Friday	
Tuesday		Saturday	
Wednesday		Sunday	
Thursday			

El Condor Pasa   by Simon and Garfunkel

1. a) Read the text below. As you listen to the song underline the words that are incorrect.
   b) Listen to the song again. Write the correct word on the lines given. (Tip: You will find the correct words at the bottom of the page.)

I'd rather be a rabbit than a cat. _____
Yes I would. _____
If I could, _____
I surely would. Hmmm ... _____

I'd rather be a lorry than a bus. _____
Yes I would. _____
If I only could, _____
I surely would. Hmmm ... _____

Away, I'd rather kick a ball _____
Like a swan that's here and gone. _____
A dog gets tied up to the tree. _____
He gives the park its saddest sound, _____
Its saddest sound. Hmmm ... _____

I'd rather be a teacher than a class. _____
Yes I would. _____
If I could, _____
I surely would. _____

I'd rather feel the bed beneath my head. _____
Yes I would. _____
If I only could _____
I surely would. _____

© 1933 / 1963 / 1970 by Edward B. Marks Music Co., for D: Musikverlag Intersong GmbH, Hamburg

sparrow — snail — earth — hammer — man — sail away — ground — nail — world — street — forest — feet

2. a) **Work in a group. Ask your classmates the questions below and write the answers into the grid. You can ask them to give reasons for their answers, too.**

Who	
Which thing	would you like to be? / (+)
What animal	would you not like to be? (−)
Where	

Name	Person	Thing	Animal	Place
	+ −	+ −	+ −	+ −
	+ −	+ −	+ −	+ −
	+ −	+ −	+ −	+ −
	+ −	+ −	+ −	+ −
	+ −	+ −	+ −	+ −

b) **Report your results to the rest of the class. Make sentences like:**
John would rather be Michael Jackson than Elton John.

c) **Make an "I'd rather be ... than ..." poster showing your own answers.**

3. **Imagine you had a dream last night. In it you were someone else, or a thing, or you were in a different place. The dream can be nice / terrible / exciting. Write about the dream.**

Our House by Madness

1. Fill in the missing sentences.

Father wears his Sunday best
Mother's tired, she needs a rest

Sister's sighing in her sleep
Brother's got a date to keep

Our house, in the middle of our street
Our house in the middle of our ...

Our house it has a crowd
There's always something happening

Our mum she's so house-proud

And a mess is not allowed.

Our house, in the middle of our street
Our house in the middle of our ... (2)
Something tells you that you've got to get away from it.

Mother has to iron his shirt

Sees them off with a small kiss
She's the one they're going to miss in lots of ways.

Our house, in the middle of our street
Our house, in the middle of our ...

I remember way back then when everything was true
And when we would have such a very good time
Such a fine time

And I remember how we'd play simply waste the day away
Then we'd say nothing would come between us two dreamers.

Father wears his Sunday best
Mother's tired she needs a rest
The kids are playing up downstairs
Sister's sighing in her sleep
Brother's got a date to keep
He can't hang around.

Our house, in the middle of our street (3)
Our house in the middle of our ...

Our house was our castle and our keep
Our house in the middle of our street
Our house that was where we used to sleep
Our house in the middle of our street.

The kids are playing up downstairs   *He can't hang around.*
Then she sends the kids to school   *Father gets up late for work*
Such a happy time   *Nothing ever slows her down*   *And it's usually quite loud*

2. **Can you crack the code to find the mystery place and the famous person who lives there? Fit the words at the bottom of the page into the grid. Then work out who the person is and where they live.**
   Tip: Each number corresponds to a letter of the alphabet (1=s). Write in the letters under the numbers as you fill in the grid.

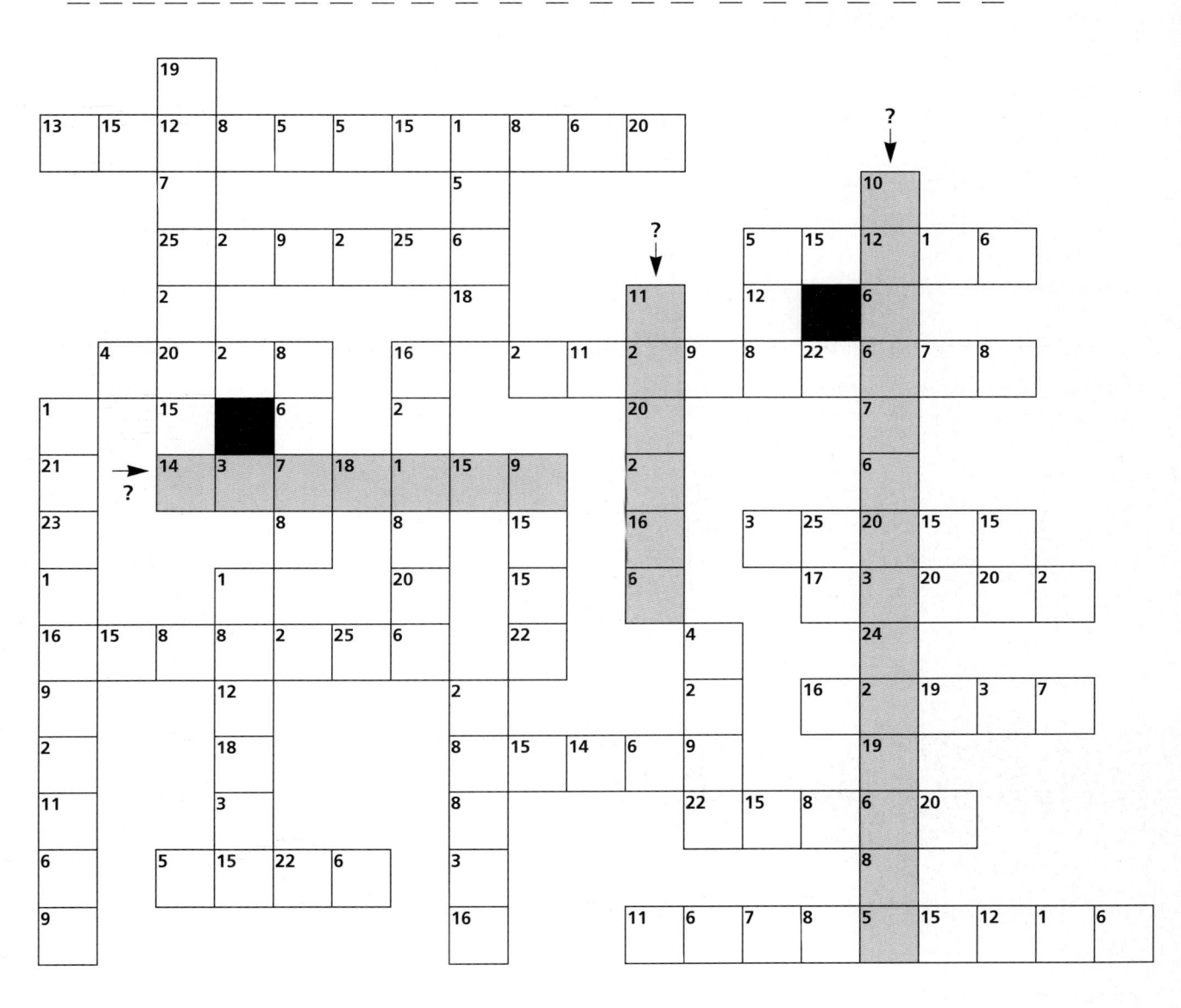

```
 1  2  3  4  5  6  7  8  9 10 11 12 13 14 15 16 17 18 19 20 21 22 23 24
 S  _  _  _  _  _  _  _  _  _  _  _  _  _  _  _  _  _  _  _  _  _  _  _
```

3 letters
hut

4 letters
farm
flat
home
room
shed
tent

5 letters
attic
cabin
house
igloo
motel
tower
villa

6 letters
castle
garage
studio

7 letters
cottage

8 letters
bungalow

9 letters
apartment
penthouse

10 letters
skyscraper

11 letters
youth hostel

25

3. a) Put all the words you think of when you hear the word *house* into the mind map below.

$$\text{House}$$

b) Look at the words in your mind map and try to make rhyming pairs. For example:

   wall – small   new – blue   door – floor

c) With a partner, write a rap about a house with the rhyming pairs. Why not start like this: *My house is blue / It's big, untidy and new...* Now take your time and start to rhyme!

4. Write five sentences about your dream house. What rooms has it got? What is in the rooms? Draw a picture of your room in the dream house in the box.

_____
_____
_____
_____
_____

Jeans On by Dave Dundas

1. a) Can you put the letters into the right order to make words?

E A N S J ☐	G U A T I R ☐	N S N U Y ☐	G T I R E ☐
....	....	....	....

O C E L S ☐	A L C E P ☐	D E N W E K T ☐	B I O R G N ☐
....	....	....	....

L D A O R L ☐	O I R M G N N ☐	R A T I H L G ☐	C K O P E T ☐
....	....	....	....

b) Which of the words in the boxes are in the song, too? Tick the box ✔ when you hear a word.

2. As you listen to the song, fill in the missing words. (Tip: The words are in task 1, too.)

When I wake up
In the _____ light
I pull on my jeans
And I feel _____
I pull my blue jeans on
I pull my old blue jeans on
I pull my blue jeans on
I pull my old blue jeans on

It's the _____
And I know that you're free
So pull on your jeans
And come on out with me
(I need to have you near me
I need to feel you _____ to me: 2)

You and me
We'll go motorbike-riding
In the sun and the wind and the rain
I got money in my _____
Got a _____ in my tank
And I'm King of the Road again.

I'll meet ya in the usual _____
I don't need a thing
Except your pretty face
(And I need to have you near me
I need to feel you close to me: 2)

You and me
We'll go.......

© by Air Music London Ltd., für D, A, CH: EMI Music Publishing Gemany GmbH, Hamburg

3. Fill in the names of the pieces of clothing next to the numbers in the puzzle.

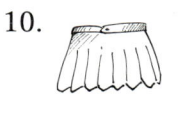

1. 
2. 
3. 
4. 
5.  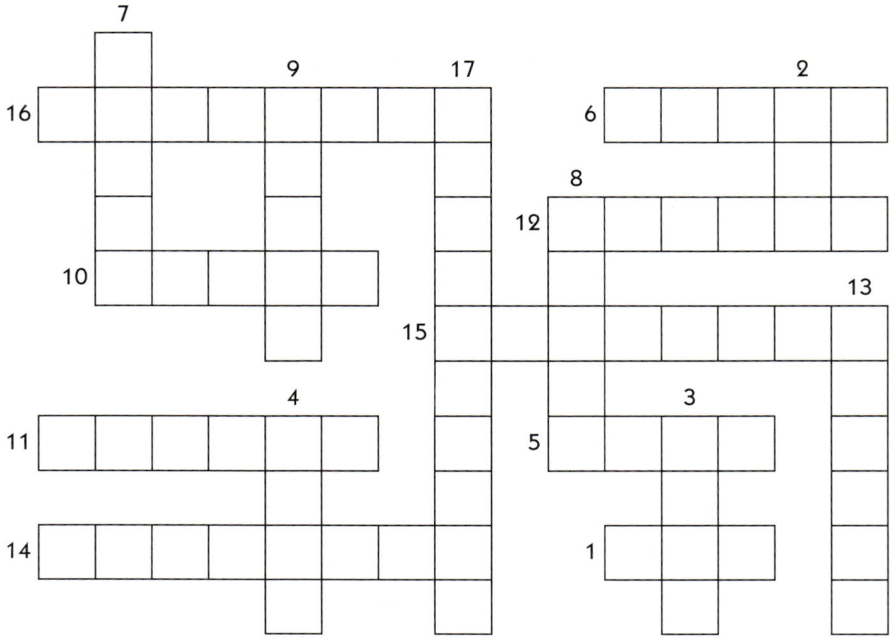
6. 
7. 
8.
9. 
10.
11. 
12.
13. 
14.
15. 
16.
17.

4. Partner A
   – Colour in the clothes in Picture 1. Describe Picture 1 to your partner.
   – Partner B will tell you what colours he/she used in Picture 2. Colour in Picture 2 based on what your partner says.
   – Compare your pictures.

✂ -

Partner B
   – Colour in the clothes in Picture 1. Describe Picture 1 to your partner.
   – Partner A will tell you what colours he/she used in Picture 2. Colour in Picture 2 based on what your partner says.
   – Compare your pictures.

June Afternoon by Roxette

**1. a) Listen to the song and underline the extra word in each line.
b) Write the extra words on the lines given. Put the first letter of each word into the phrase below to make up "a nice thing to have on a June afternoon".**

Didn't I always tell you everything is possible in this déjà vu? 1. _____

Try the riverboat, the carousel, feed the happy pigeons, barbecue 2. _____

Look at all the old people, happy faces all around. 3. _____

Smiling, throwing kisses then, busy making lazy sounds 4. _____

It's a bright silly June afternoon, 5. _____

It usually never gets dark. (Wah, wah!) 6. _____

Here comes the sun now. 7. _____

Get your new green green tambourine, 8. _____

Yes, let's play in the park. (Wah, wah!) 9. _____

And here comes the sun. 10. _____

Some folks are on free blankets, slowly daydreaming 11. _____

And reaching for their terrible food. 12. _____

Let's go buy an easy ice-cream and a magazine 13. _____

Right with an attitude 14. _____

And never put on a cassette, 15. _____

We can only pretend that you're a star 16. _____

'Cause our life's so very simple 17. _____

Not just like la-la-la. 18. _____

It's in a bright June afternoon, 19. _____

It nearly never gets dark. (Wah, wah!) 20. _____

Hello! Here comes the sun. 21. _____

Get your green green yellow tambourine, 22. _____

Let's play in the dirty park. (Wah, wah!) 23. _____

Here comes the evening sun, comes the sun. 24. _____

There's a poor painter painting his masterpiece. 25. _____

There are some squirrels all jumping in the trees. 26. _____

There's a wide-eyed boy with a red red balloon. 27. _____

All my life I've longed for this afternoon, Kate. [...] 28. _____

Solution: ___ ___ ___ ___ ___ ___ ___ ___ ___
 1   2   3   4   5   6   7   8   9

___ ___ ___ ___ ___ ___ ___ ___ ___   ___ ___ ___ ___ ___ ___   ___ ___ ___ ___
10 11 12 13 14 15 16 17 18   19 20 21 22 23 24   25 26 27 28

2. What things, animals, people and activities do you associate with a park? Write your ideas into the mind map.

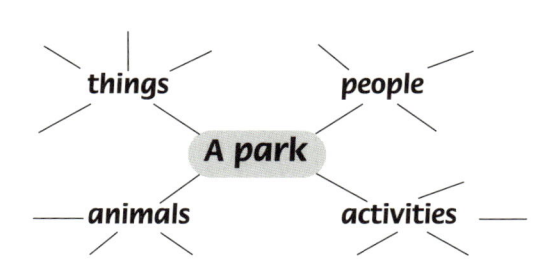

```
      things         people
             \      /
            A park
             /      \
      animals       activities
```

3. a) Describe what is going on in the picture. You can use words from exercises 1 and 2.
   b) What do you think the people having the barbecue are saying to each other? With a partner, write a conversation between two of the people.

4. Follow the instructions and write a diamond poem about a month of the year.

a) Write down the name of a month.   a) _____
b) Give two adjectives to describe the
   month.   b) _____
c) Think of three things you often do in
   that month. Write down their ing-   c) _____
   forms.
d) Write down two adjectives to show   d) _____
   how you feel then.
e) Repeat the name of the month.   e) _____

Lemon Tree   by Fool's Garden

1. Listen to the song and fill in the missing words.

go

see

want

I'm sitting here in a boring _____
It's just another rainy Sunday _____
I'm wasting my time
I got nothing to _____
I'm hanging around
I'm _____ for you
But nothing ever happens – and I wonder

I'm driving around in my _____
I'm driving too fast, I'm driving too far
I'd _____ to change my point of view
I feel so lonely, I'm waiting for you
But nothing ever happens – and I wonder

CHORUS: I wonder how I wonder why
_____ you told me 'bout the blue blue sky
and all that I can _____ is just a yellow lemon tree
I'm turning my _____ up and down
I'm turning turning turning turning turning around
And all that I can see is just a yellow lemon tree

room

Sing da ... dee da ...

toy

I'm _____ here, I miss the power
I'd like to _____ out taking a shower
But there's a heavy cloud inside my head
I feel so tired, put myself into _____
Where nothing ever happens – and I wonder

waiting

Isolation – is not _____ for me
Isolation – I don't _____ to sit on a lemon tree
I'm steppin' around in a desert of joy
Maybe anyhow I'll get another _____
And everything will happen – and you'll wonder

bed

CHORUS

car

like

head

sitting

afternoon

yesterday

do

good

© 1995 by EMI MMC Musikverlag GmbH & Co. KG, Hamburg.

2. **Play the following game with 2–3 of your classmates.**

> *How to play:*
> - *Cut out the cards.*
> - *Each player has a certain number of cards. You decide how many!*
> - *The idea is to make full sentences (= three or four cards!). You can make silly sentences, too, but they must be correct.*
> - *The first player puts down a card and the others take turns adding more cards.*
> - *When a player finishes a sentence, he or she gets those cards.*
> - *The player with the most cards at the end of the game is the winner.*

my mother	across the sea	are playing	in the city centre
are singing	the children	in the bathroom	on the table
a budgie	a tennis match	the boys	is talking
in the street	for Sally	is reading	the girls
sweets	are having	Sarah	a book
are writing	Tom	to my teacher	are putting
some pupils	is eating	in the park	is listening to
am flying	the old lady	through the air	the hamster
behind the house	are cleaning	the dog	in the pet shop
on TV	on the phone	is taking	the cat
is barking	a song	my father	is buying

you	the woman	for a walk	the car
many people	is sailing	is sleeping	at school
is playing	my friends	in the classroom	is buying
out of the cage	in the snackbar	John	football
lunch	are waiting	our garden	grandfather
in the kitchen	to a CD	I	are watching
is taking	he	the guitar	on the balcony
a ghost story	in my balloon	at the cat	home
under a tree	she	the rabbit	a hamburger

3. Play the game with 2-3 classmates.

How to play:
- You need one dice and a counter for each player.
- Cut out the 24 activity cards (you can make more cards, too!) and put them in a pile face down on the table.
- The first person throws the dice to take a turn.
- If you land on a ? you must take one of the cards. You must say what the people in the picture are doing. If your sentence is correct, you go up the ladder (↑). If it is wrong, you must go back down (↓) the ladder.
- If you land on a 😐 you miss a turn.
- If you land on a 😀 you can throw the dice again.

EXAMPLE: The man is playing football.

34

START
1
2
3
4
5
6
7
8
9
10
11
12
13
14
15
16
17
18
19
20
21
22
23
24
25
26
27
28
29
30
31
32
33
34
35
36
37
38
39
40
41
42
43
44
45
46
47
48
49
50
51
52
53
54
FINISH

I Can't Help Myself by The Kelly Family

1. **Read the list of verbs and tick (✔) the ones you hear in the song. How many verbs did you get?**

be		kiss		talk	
change		like		tell	
come		listen		think	
do		love		turn	
give		read		wait	
hate		say		walk	
have		see		want	
hear		stand		watch	
help		stop		wish	
hold		take		write	

2. **Make up a new verse from the point of view of the singer's ex-girlfriend. You could start with:** *"But I can't …"* **or** *"I wanna …"*.

_____

_____

_____

_____

_____

_____

Respect Yourself by DJ BoBo

1 a) Can you match the words in the box that rhyme? The first one has been done for you.

> pray   know   blind   free   hide → aim
> resignation   isolation
> game ← inside   mind   way   rainbow   destiny

b) Listen to the song and use the rhyming words to complete the gaps in the text.

Respect yourself
Respect yourself
Don't run away
Respect yourself
Respect yourself
Come on help each other out
And respect yourself

You don't know, no, what you don't _____
I like the colors of the _____
Respect is the name of the _____
Respect yourself
And you never miss your _____
If your show weakness
You gotta let them know
You don't know, no, what you don't know
If you wanna grow, say no, just go

Chorus:
Respect yourself
Change your _____
Respect yourself
Don't be _____
Respect yourself
And you will see the light
Respect yourself
And you will find your _____
So practise what you _____
Don't run away
Respect yourself
Respect yourself (2)
You will see the light

Don't care about what people say
Believe in yourself and go your own way

Respect, no _____
Leave the path of _____
Don't care about what people say
R.E.S.P.E.C.T. will never get away
Today, we stay, and pay attention anyway
Fair play, every day, don't run away

Change your mind
Don't be blind
And you will see the light
And you will find your way
So practise what you pray
Don't run away
Respect yourself

Chorus

If you're feeling weak so deep _____
No place to run, no place to _____
R.E.S.P.E.C.T.
Respect your _____
If you don't know what is right or wrong
If you feel confused and your thoughts are gone
R.E.S.P.E.C.T.
Respect yourself, be _____

Respect yourself (2)
So practise what you pray
You will see the light (2)

Chorus

Respect yourself (5)
You will see the light
Respect yourself (3)
Don't run away
Respect yourself

© Edition Capricorn – EAMS Musikverlag, Bishop Songs Musikverlag

2. **Listen to the song again. Then write any words or phrases that came to mind into the mind map below.**

RESPECT YOURSELF

3. **Now do *one* of the following tasks.**
   a) Complete this poem. You could use some of the rhyming pairs you found in task 1.

Respect yourself
Don't _____
Don't _____
Don't _____
Don't _____
Don't _____
Don't _____
Don't _____
Respect yourself

b) Write a poem in which you say how you respect yourself and others. Try to make your poem rhyme.

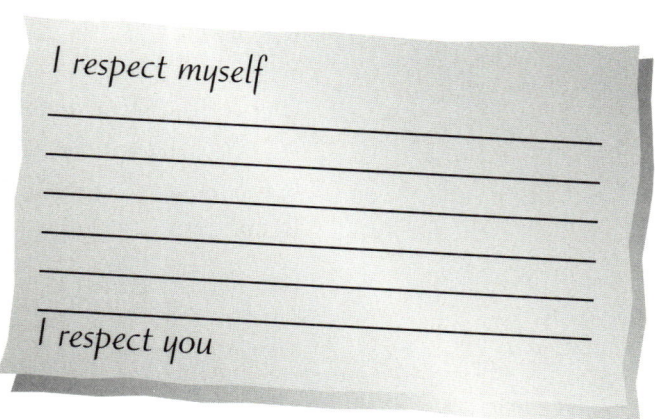

I respect myself
_____
_____
_____
_____
_____
I respect you

c) Write a poem using the letters in the word *RESPECT*. Here is an example with "love":

L et's dance in the street
O ur hearts beat
V anilla ice cream and apple pie
E very day till we die

38

The World in Perfect State   by Hessel

1. Cut out the parts of the song. Listen to the song and put the parts into the correct order.

No one in the world can help me more
To make the sand so white
The water shines bright
And the sky is right

Chorus
_____

The water's blue, blue and green
The sand so white you've never seen
The sky so clean
It's too long ago
That we had the feeling

Chorus
_____

What it's supposed to be
A place that's great to be
A clean beach baby, for you and me
Yeah that's the right way

Garbage, beaches, dirty water
Filthy skies and no excuse
For what we did
It's the work we have

Chorus
_____

Why there's a good way
Yeah, that's the good way

Now the world is tired
Carry our dirt day after day
Year after year, why it's the bad way
Yeah, it's the bad way

Chorus
I like to see the world in perfect state
Like you to meet me on a place that's great
I like to live on a place that's nice and cosy
I like to see the world in perfect state
Why there's a good way
Yeah, that's the good way

How it's real, now it's the dirt
That really hurts
Oh, it's the bad way
Yeah, it's the bad way

Chorus
_____

Why that's the good way
Yeah, that's the good way

© Groene Weide Muziek BV, Terschelling Hoorn.

2. **Here is the homepage of a New Zealand website. It is for kids who care about our world. Read about Brucie and his friends in Southland, New Zealand.**

BRUCIE'S BUDDIES
kids caring for the environment

WELCOME TO BRUCIE'S BUDDIES HOMEPAGE!!
Bruce's Buddies in the Southland Regional Council's own club for
"Kids Caring For The Environment"
It's FREE for kids in the Southland Region and is Southland's largest kid's club.
If you're not a member, but would like to know more, contact:
Environmental Education Officer
Southland Regional Council
Private Bag 90116
Invercargill
New Zealand

ALBERT T. ROSS

Albert is Brucie's cousin and lives at Campbell Island. He helps people to
Care for Our Coast.

ELLIE EEL

Ellie lives in the rivers, streams, lakes and estuaries of Southland. She wants people to
Respect Our Rivers.

TESSA TUI

Tessa lives in our forests and native bush. She would like people to
Treasure Our Trees.

3. **Project: Brucie loves getting mail and has now learned how to use e-mail! You can write to Brucie and he will write back to you as soon as he returns to his nest. Here is his e-mail address:**

   buddies@brucecgull.com

4. **Storytime: Brucie and his friends protecting the rivers**
   a) You and your partner have got four different pictures of the story. Describe the first picture to your partner, (e.g. *In the first picture there is/there are...*).
   b) Partner B then describes the picture he/she thinks is the second part of the story.
   c) Then you describe the picture that you think describes the third part of the story and so on.
   d) When you have finished the story you can cut out the pictures and put them in the right order.

Partner A   Picture 1

4. Storytime: Brucie and his friends protecting the rivers

a) You and your partner have each got four different pictures of a story. Partner A describes the first picture to you.

b) You describe the picture you think is the second part of the story (e.g. *In the second picture Brucie says "…"*).

c) Then Partner A describes the picture he/she thinks is the third part of the story and so on.

d) When you have finished the story, you can cut out the pictures and put them in the right order with your partner.

Partner B

Simon Says by 1910 Fruitgum Co.

1. a) Listen to the song and number the verses in the order you hear them.

O | Now that you have learned to play this game with me
You can see it's not so hard to do
Let's try it once again, this time more carefully
And I hope the winner will be you

C | Simple Simon says – Put your hands on your hips
Let your backbone slip – Simon says
Simple Simon says – Put your hands on your hips
Let your backbone slip – Simon says

N | Clap your hands in the air – Simple Simon says
Do it double time – Simple Simon says
Slow it down like before – Simple Simon says
Are you looking fine? – Simple Simon says

A | Put your hands in the air – Simple Simon says
Shake them all about – Simple Simon says
Do it when Simon says –
And you will never be out.

E | Now clap them high in the air – Simple Simon says
Do it double time – Simple Simon says
Slow it down like before – Simple Simon says
Are you looking fine?

B | Put your hands on your head – Simple Simon says
Bring them down by your side – Simple Simon says
Shake them to your left – Simple Simon says
Now shake them to your right

B | I'd like to play a game that is so much fun
And it's not so very hard to do
The name of the game is Simple Simon Says
And I would like for you to play it too.

K | Put your hands on your head – Simple Simon says
Bring them down by your side – Simple Simon says
Shake them to your left – Simple Simon says
Now shake them to your right

b) When you have put the verses in the correct order, make a new word with the letters that go with each verse.
Write the word here: 1 2 3 4 5 6 7 8
  __ __ __ __ __ __ __ __

2. a) Underline the sentences in which Simple Simon tells you what actions to do.
b) Think of six more actions and write them on the lines below.

_____   _____

_____   _____

_____   _____

3. a) **There are 15 parts of the body hidden in the grid below. Can you find them?**

→ 4 words   ↑ 2 words   ↓ 4 words   ← 2 words   ↘ 2 words   ↗ 1 word

F	R	H	A	N	D	M	I	T	H	A	M
A	H	E	G	F	I	N	G	E	R	L	R
C	H	A	I	Y	A	L	O	D	Z	E	A
E	G	D	O	B	E	N	M	S	A	L	E
M	K	K	S	G	E	I	R	C	E	B	A
B	L	N	M	O	U	T	H	A	R	O	T
R	R	O	E	V	E	T	O	O	F	W	O
O	A	G	R	E	T	C	Y	A	S	E	E
N	E	Y	E	F	R	K	C	E	N	A	T

b) **Now draw a picture of a person and label it with the words you found in the grid.**

Top Of The World (Olé, Olé, Olé)

by Chumbawamba

1. Listen to the song and write in the missing words from the list below.

Words on a postcard from far away
Spoke of a time long ago
Laughed ourselves daft on that Saturday
Singing "Here We Go"…

I'm a taxi _____
I'm a postal _____
I'm an office _____
I'm a striking docker
I'm a ballet _____
I'm a zapatista
I'm a pop _____
I'm a winner –
I'm a winner, baby
I'm a winner, baby

Chorus *(sung twice)*:
Olé, Olé, Olé
Top of the world
I'm on top of the world…

I'm a bricklayer
I'm an ex-_____
I'm a single _____
I'm a bus _____
I'm a political prisoner
I'm a print _____
I'm a foot _____
I'm a winner –
I'm a winner, baby
I'm a winner, baby

Chorus: Olé, Olé, Olé
Top of the world
I'm on top of the world…

miner *driver* *worker* *cleaner* *singer* *dancer* *mother* *worker* *driver* *-baller*

© 1998 by Hans Kusters Music N.V., für D, A, CH: EMI Music Publishing Germany GmbH, Hamburg/ Richard Kaun Musikverlag KG, Munich.

2. **Match the words on the left with the words on the right. Then write the correct word under the pictures.**

1. American	skiing
2. ice	riding
3. table	skating
4. downhill	ball
5. horse	football
6. wind	tennis
7. high	lifting
8. basket	hockey
9. roller	jump
10. weight	surfing

3. **Find 15 different sports (→, ↓, ↑, ←) in the grid below.**

B	A	S	K	E	T	B	A	L	L	H	M	T	T
V	C	U	G	T	E	D	P	Q	G	O	H	C	G
H	R	V	N	E	L	X	A	P	N	C	S	Q	O
D	I	V	I	N	G	Q	V	M	I	K	X	J	K
Y	C	T	L	N	O	P	G	G	M	E	E	D	D
B	K	S	C	I	T	S	A	N	M	Y	G	X	C
G	E	G	Y	S	N	O	T	N	I	M	D	A	B
U	T	C	C	G	C	Z	F	O	W	G	O	L	F
R	H	Q	D	G	N	I	I	K	S	P	V	I	I
Z	U	Z	R	D	R	E	C	C	O	S	P	I	Y
X	B	O	D	U	J	S	A	I	L	I	N	G	P

4. **Play a memory game with your classmates. Cut out the cards, turn them over and mix them up. The person to get the most matching pairs is the winner.**

47

cricket	table tennis	weight lifting	tennis
cycling	sailing	football	wind-surfing
ice-hockey	skate-boarding	boxing	running
American football	high jump	skiing	ice-skating
golf	horse riding	baseball	basketball

What A Wonderful World

by Louis Armstrong

I see trees of green, red roses, too
I see them bloom for me and you,
And I think to myself: What a wonderful world!
I see skies of blue and clouds of white,
The bright blessed day, the dark sacred night,
And I think to myself: What a wonderful world!

The colours of the rainbow, so pretty in the sky,
Are also on the faces of people goin' by.
I see friends shakin' hands, sayin' "How do you do?"
They're really sayin' "I love you."

I hear babies cry, I watch them grow,
They'll learn much more than I'll ever know,
And I think to myself: What a wonderful world!
And I think to myself: What a wonderful world!
Yeah, I think to myself, what a wonderful world

© Abilene Music Corp. / Herald Square Music Co., für D, A, CH: Melodie der Welt, J. Michel KG, Musikverlag, Frankfurt / Eldorado Musikverlag GmbH, Hamburg.

---

1. Draw a colourful picture of a wonderful world.

A wonderful world

2. a) In the first verse of the song the singer mentions four different colours. Listen carefully and write down the colours in the order you hear them.
b) Then use the colours to colour in the T-shirt correctly.

1st. colour: _____

2nd. colour: _____

3rd. colour: _____

4th. colour: _____

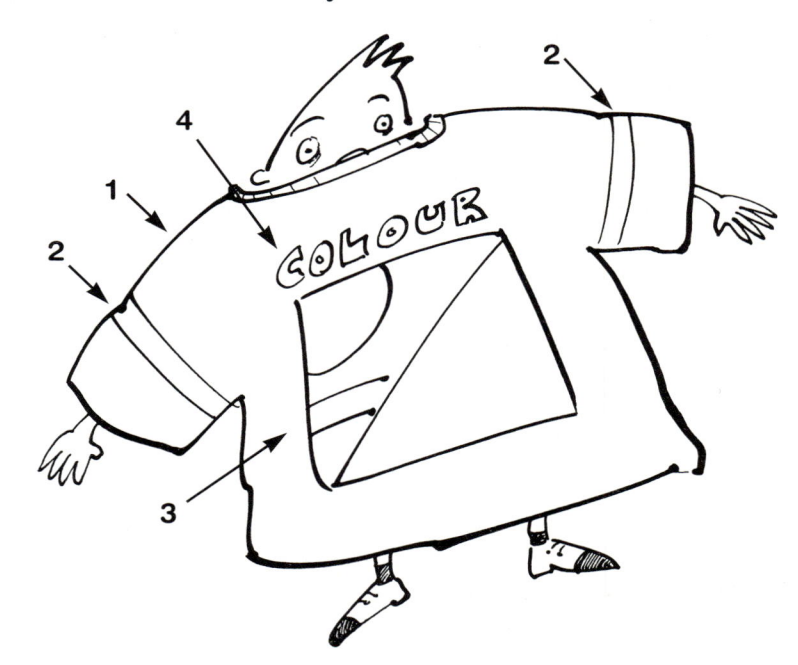

3. Listen to the song again and tick the words you hear.

> faces   hens   colours   night   room   people   tea   pupils
> trees   friends   rainbow   hands   roses   say   sea
> day   right   rabbits   clouds   babies

4. The singer uses many adjectives to describe what he sees. Read the text and mark the adjectives. Write them down in the table below with the word they describe.

adjectives	words

5. Match the adjectives on the left with their opposites on the right. Write down the pairs. Then write down more pairs of adjectives.

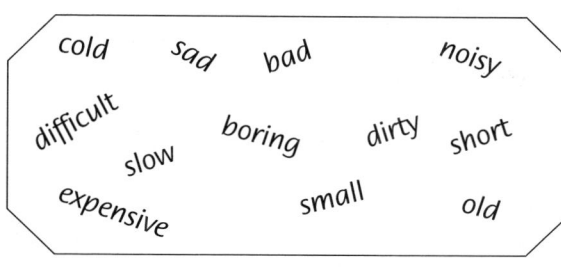

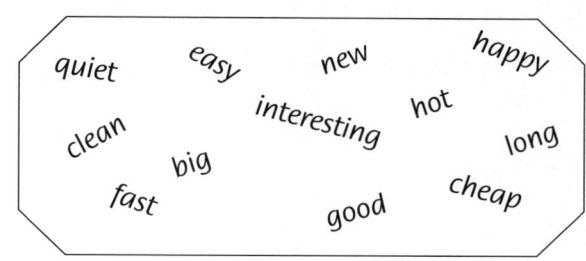

cold   sad   bad   noisy   difficult   boring   dirty   short   slow   expensive   small   old

quiet   easy   new   happy   clean   interesting   hot   big   long   fast   good   cheap

1. _____
2. _____
3. _____
4. _____
5. _____
6. _____
7. _____
8. _____
9. _____
10. _____
11. _____
12. _____

Other pairs of adjectives _____
_____

6. Use colourful adjectives to describe one of these places: your room – your home – your school.

_____
_____
_____
_____
_____
_____

7. In the second verse the singer talks about friends who meet in the street and shake hands. Imagine and write down a dialogue between two friends.

_____
_____
_____
_____
_____
_____
_____

**8. Make up a story using some of the following pairs of words:
dark morning – red clouds – big spaceship – broken computer – long journey – green men – big surprise – warm welcome – sad goodbye.
Write your story on a big piece of paper and draw a picture to go with it.**

Words by Boyzone

1. Write in the missing lines. You must use some lines more than once.

Smile an everlasting smile
_____

Don't ever let me find you gone
'Cause that would bring a tear to me

This world has lost its glory
_____

> I'm here if you should call to me

> It's only words

Now my love

You think that I don't even mean
_____

It's only words
And words are all I have
_____

> And words are all I have

Talk in everlasting words
And dedicate them all to me
And I will give you all my life
_____

> Let's start a brand-new story

You think that I don't even mean
_____

> A single word I say

It's only words
_____

> To take your heart away

To take your heart away

It's only words
_____

> A smile can bring you near to me

To take your heart away
Da da ...

You think that I don't even mean
_____

It's only words
And words are all I have
To take your heart away *("You think..." is repeated two more times.)*

© by Gibb Brothers Music Inc. Ltd. für D, A, CH: Music-Edition Discoton GmbH (BMG UFA Musikverlage), München.

2. Play *Word Bingo* with your classmates.
- Cut out the word cards and put them on the table. All of the words have to do with *school*.
- Each player writes down ten of the words on his/her bingo card.
- The word cards are put into a box. One pupil takes out the cards one by one. He/she calls out the words.
- The players tick the words as they are called. The first player to tick all of the words on his/her card is the winner. He/she can call out the words the next time.

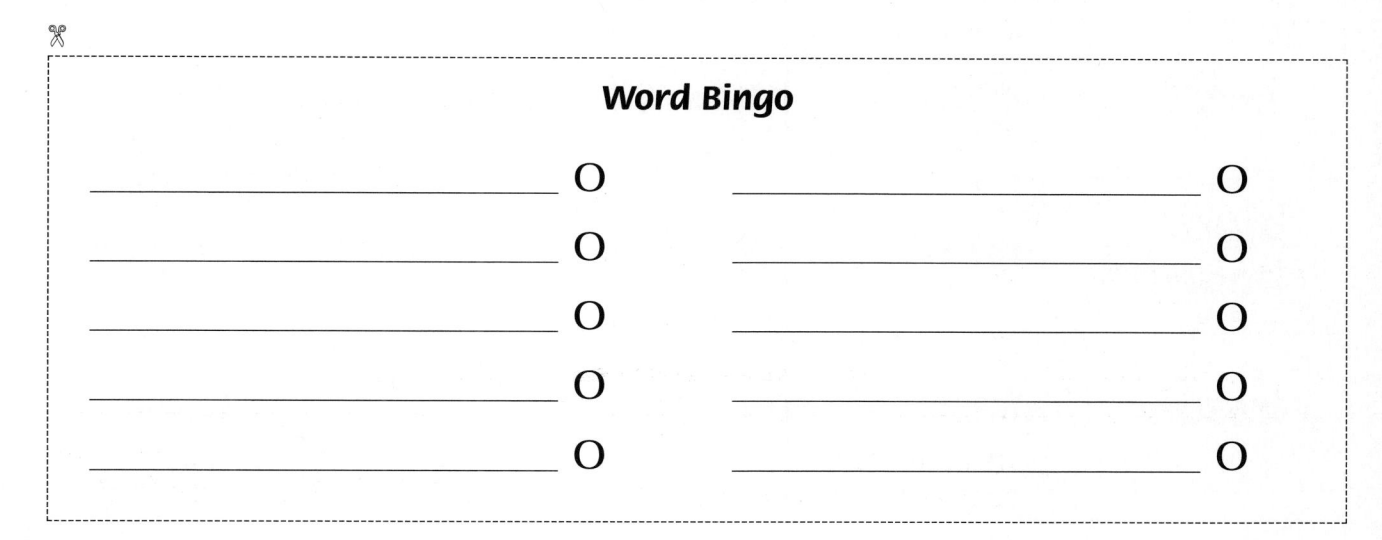

Word Bingo

_____ O   _____ O
_____ O   _____ O
_____ O   _____ O
_____ O   _____ O
_____ O   _____ O

You can make your own bingo word games about other topics. Before you make the word cards, collect words in a mind map. Then write the words on cards. Here are two mind maps to start you off.

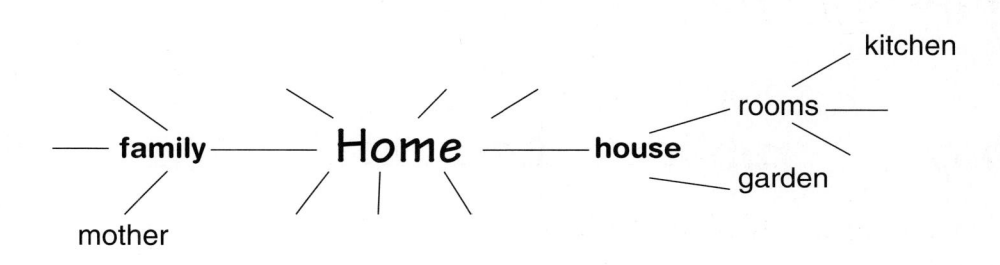

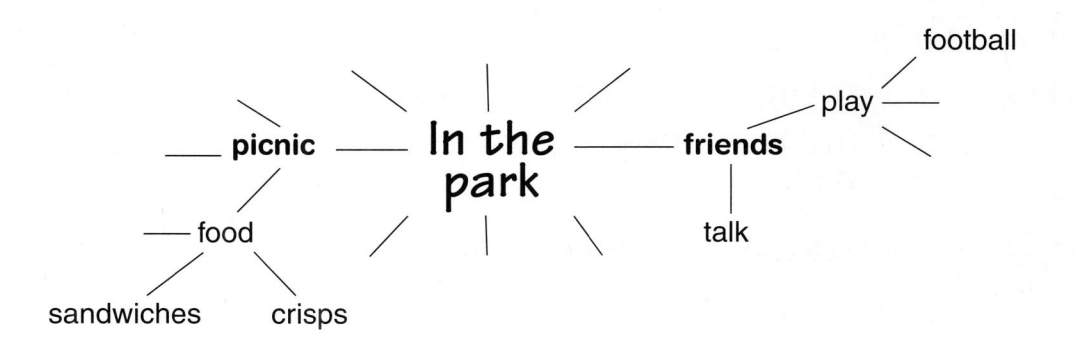

family — **Home** — house — rooms — kitchen / garden
mother

picnic — **In the park** — friends — play — football
food — sandwiches / crisps
talk

uniform	group	felt-tip pen	Sports	late
break	desk	school-bag	Music	ill
lunch	chair	register	calculator	eat
blackboard	chalk	workbook	assembly	play
lesson	duster	homework	school club	sing
teacher	map	page	rules	count
pupil	book	English	test	learn
boy	rubber	German	subject	boring
girl	ruler	Biology	read	interesting
class	pencil	Maths	write	picture
atlas	pen	Science	draw	story
partner	biro	timetable	work	exercise

Macarena (Bayside Boys Remix) by Los Del Rio

Draw pictures of yourself doing the actions to "Macarena".

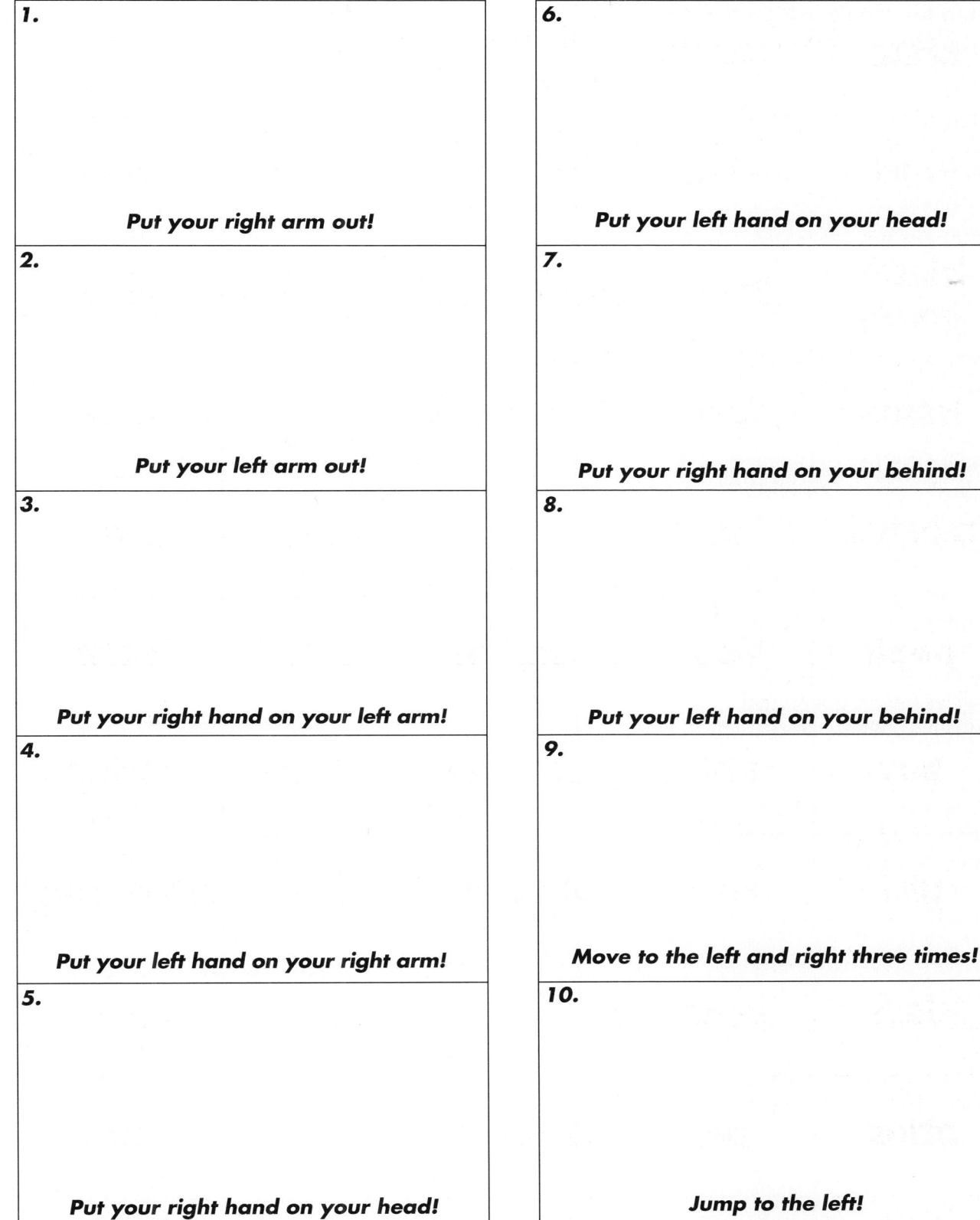

1. Put your right arm out!
2. Put your left arm out!
3. Put your right hand on your left arm!
4. Put your left hand on your right arm!
5. Put your right hand on your head!
6. Put your left hand on your head!
7. Put your right hand on your behind!
8. Put your left hand on your behind!
9. Move to the left and right three times!
10. Jump to the left!

Start again at the beginning!

YMCA by Village People

1. a) Read the text below and try to guess what the missing words are. Write your ideas into the blanks with a pencil first.
b) Listen to the song and check your answers.

Young man, there's no need to feel _____
I said, young man, pick yourself off the ground
I said, young man, 'cause you're in a new town
There's no need to be _____.

Young man, there's a place you can _____
I said, young man, when you're short on your dough
You can stay there, and I'm sure you will find
Many ways to have a good _____.

Chorus: It's fun to stay at the YMCA
It's fun to stay at the YMCA
They have everything for young men to enjoy
You can hang out with all the boys.

It's fun to stay at the YMCA
It's fun to stay at the YMCA
You can get yourself clean
You can have a good meal
You can do whatever you _____.

Young man, are you listening to _____?
I said, young man, what do you want to be?
I said, young man, you can make real your dreams,
But you've got to know this one _____.

No man does it all by himself
I said, young man, put your pride on the _____
And just go there, to the YMCA
I'm sure they can help you _____.

Chorus: It's fun to stay at the YMCA
It's fun to stay at the YMCA
They have everything for young men to enjoy.
You can hang out with all the boys.
It's fun to stay at the YMCA
It's fun to stay at the YMCA
You can get yourself clean
You can have a good meal
You can do whatever you _____.

Young man, I was once in your _____,
I said, I was down and out with the blues
I felt, no man cared if I were alive
I felt the whole world was so jive.

That's when someone came up to me
And said young man take a walk up the _____
There's a place there called the YMCA
They can start you back on your _____.

It's fun to stay at the YMCA
It's fun to stay at the YMCA
Young man, young man there's no need to feel _____
Young man, young man, pick yourself off the ground.

YMCA, just go to the YMCA

Sung by the Village People © 1978 by Scorpio Music, France, for Germany and Austria and Switzerland, A La Carte Music Verlags-GmbH, Hennef.

2. Find 22 verbs (→, ↑) in the grid. (Tip: The verbs are in the song, too.)

F	E	E	L	I	S	O	P	U	T	Y
I	N	N	I	S	T	O	L	P	C	E
N	O	R	S	T	A	R	T	E	A	N
D	I	N	T	A	Y	V	A	U	R	D
H	A	V	E	N	L	T	K	B	E	A
R	T	K	N	O	W	S	E	B	X	A
C	K	I	D	R	A	D	S	O	O	S
O	L	F	H	A	N	G	T	Z	G	A
M	A	K	E	R	T	E	N	J	O	Y
E	J	O	L	Y	V	T	A	L	S	N
G	E	D	P	I	C	K	H	D	O	T

3. Write down the verbs you found in the puzzle under the correct headings. Then write down the past tense forms. Two examples have been done for you.

regular verbs		irregular verbs	
infinitive	past tense	infinitive	past tense
pick	picked	feel	felt

4. Look at the information about activities at the Bridgwater YMCA in England. Which activities look like fun? Which wouldn't you like to do? Give reasons for your answers.
   (Tip: Visit the Bridgwater YMCA's homepage at http://ymca.org.uk/gallery/bridgwater)

Sports and Activities at the Bridgwater YMCA, England

- Skateboarding
- Computing
- Carnival Club
- Football
- Five-a-side (indoor football)
- Junior Fun Club
- Junior Roller-skating
- Kickboxing
- Line Dancing
- Roller-skating
- Youth Club

- Trips both in England and abroad
- Coffee bar
- Music
- Basketball
- Table Tennis
- Hockey
- Music
- Table Football
- TV
- Jukebox

A large number of young people come to the YMCA for the special activities at the Youth Club every Monday between 6:30 and 9:00 pm.

5. Project: *Youth groups and clubs in our town*.
   a) Make a list of the youth groups and clubs in your town.
   b) Work in small groups. Each group concentrates on one group or club on the list.
      – Collect information. (You could phone the organisers for information or go along.)
      – When you have got enough information, make a checklist about the activities offered by the group or club. See the example below.

NAME OF GROUP/CLUB:	
– when it meets	
– where it meets	
– how much it costs to join	
– who goes there	
– what you can do there / special activities	

   c) Put the checklists onto a wall chart with the heading *Youth groups and clubs in our town*.
   d) Write a personal report about one of the groups or clubs. You could write about a group or club that:
      – you already go to (say why you like it, etc.) or
      – you would like to join (say why you are interested in it).
   e) Put your report on the wall chart near the checklist for that particular group/club.

I Just Called To Say I Love You
by Stevie Wonder

1. **What ideas come to mind when you hear the word "love"? Collect your ideas in the mind map. Then compare your mind map with a classmate's.**

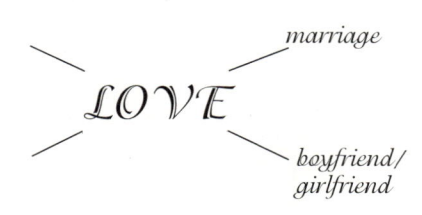

marriage
LOVE
boyfriend/girlfriend

2. **Listen to the song and tick (✓) the phrases from the song which begin with "no". Then put the lines into the order you hear them. The first one has been done for you.**

	Halloween	
	song to sing	
	bottom of my heart	
	Libra sun	
	time for birds to fly to southern skies	
	summer's high	
	autumn breeze	
	words to fill your heart	
	April rain	
✓	New Year's Day to celebrate	1
	call to say I love you	
	wedding Saturday within the month of June	
	ordinary day	
	giving thanks to all the Christmas joys you bring	
	chocolate-covered candy hearts to give away	
	though old so new	
	first of spring	
	to fill your heart	
	warm July	
	falling leaves	
	words that I must say to you	
	harvest moon to light one tender August night	
	flowers bloom	

3. Find the days, months, seasons and holidays hidden in the giant grid (→, ↑ ↓ ←).

D	T	H	A	L	L	O	W	E	E	N	S	J	U	N	E
E	A	I	M	N	A	C	K	D	P	F	F	R	I	G	H
A	B	E	T	Y	X	H	S	A	T	U	R	D	A	Y	N
S	U	Y	A	D	S	R	U	H	T	H	I	N	P	Y	E
T	Q	L	U	B	V	I	C	M	O	C	D	A	R	E	W
E	B	U	T	U	E	S	D	A	Y	R	A	N	I	C	Y
R	A	J	U	A	L	T	A	Y	T	A	Y	U	L	K	E
Y	N	G	M	J	U	M	R	E	B	M	E	C	E	D	A
A	K	I	N	D	H	A	V	E	O	C	T	O	B	E	R
D	H	C	H	R	I	S	T	M	A	S	D	A	Y	G	S
G	O	P	A	S	T	E	E	L	G	O	A	U	F	M	D
N	L	U	C	U	H	V	S	P	R	I	N	G	E	R	A
I	I	D	M	N	N	E	O	N	J	A	N	U	A	R	Y
X	D	I	D	D	R	E	T	N	I	W	K	S	A	N	D
O	A	H	I	A	T	S	U	M	M	E	R	T	H	S	Z
B	Y	G	U	Y	F	A	W	K	E	S	N	I	G	H	T

4. Write the words you found in the box under the correct headings.

– days of the week _____

_____

– months _____

_____

– seasons _____

_____

– holidays / special days _____

_____

What other words can you think of to write under each heading?

5. a) The singer talks about things that happen during the year. Which months do you associate with these things?

Halloween · harvest moon · falling leaves · Christmas joys · rain · autumn breeze · flowers bloom · birds fly to southern skies · chocolate-covered candy hearts · New Year's Day to celebrate · summer's high · first of spring

month	idea	month	idea

b) Which association do you like best? Say why and draw a picture to go with your text.

_____
_____
_____
_____
_____

6. Read the information in the box about haikus. Then write a haiku about a day, a month or a season. Draw a picture to go with your haiku.

> **Haiku**
> A haiku is a form of Japanese writing. It has three lines. The first line has five syllables, the second has seven syllables, the third line has five syllables. E.g.
> **Char / lie's / Hal / low / een**
> **He / waits / for / the / Great / Pump / kin**
> **But / he / never / comes**

Christmas Time by the Backstreet Boys

There is something special
About this time of year
A Christmas feeling's everywhere
I just got home to join you
I've been away too long
But now I'm back
To share my love
Friends are really like
One big family
Filled with love
To last throughout the year

Chorus: Christmas time, time to share our love
Come and join the tidings to the world
Christmas time, the best time of the year
Yes it's Christmas time
Christmas time ...

You and me together
Sleigh ride in the park
Loving kiss
Straight from the heart
Snowflakes falling gently
A smell of chestnuts in the air
And Christmas lights
They gleam across the sky
It's Christmas time

Chorus: Christmas time, time to share our love
Come and join the tidings to the world
Christmas time, the best time of the year
Yes it's Christmas time
Christmas time ...

Do you remember
Everything felt so nice
When I held you close to me?
Do you remember
Those cold Christmas nights
When we saw the world in harmony?

Chorus: Christmas time, time to share our love
Come and join the tidings to the world (repeated)

© by Zomba Enterprises Inc. für D, A, CH: Discoton GmbH,
(BMG UFA Musikverlage), München.

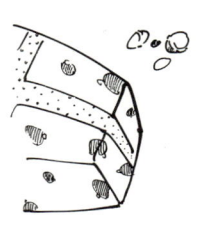

1. **Complete the Christmas crossword. (Tip: The words are given in the song text.)**

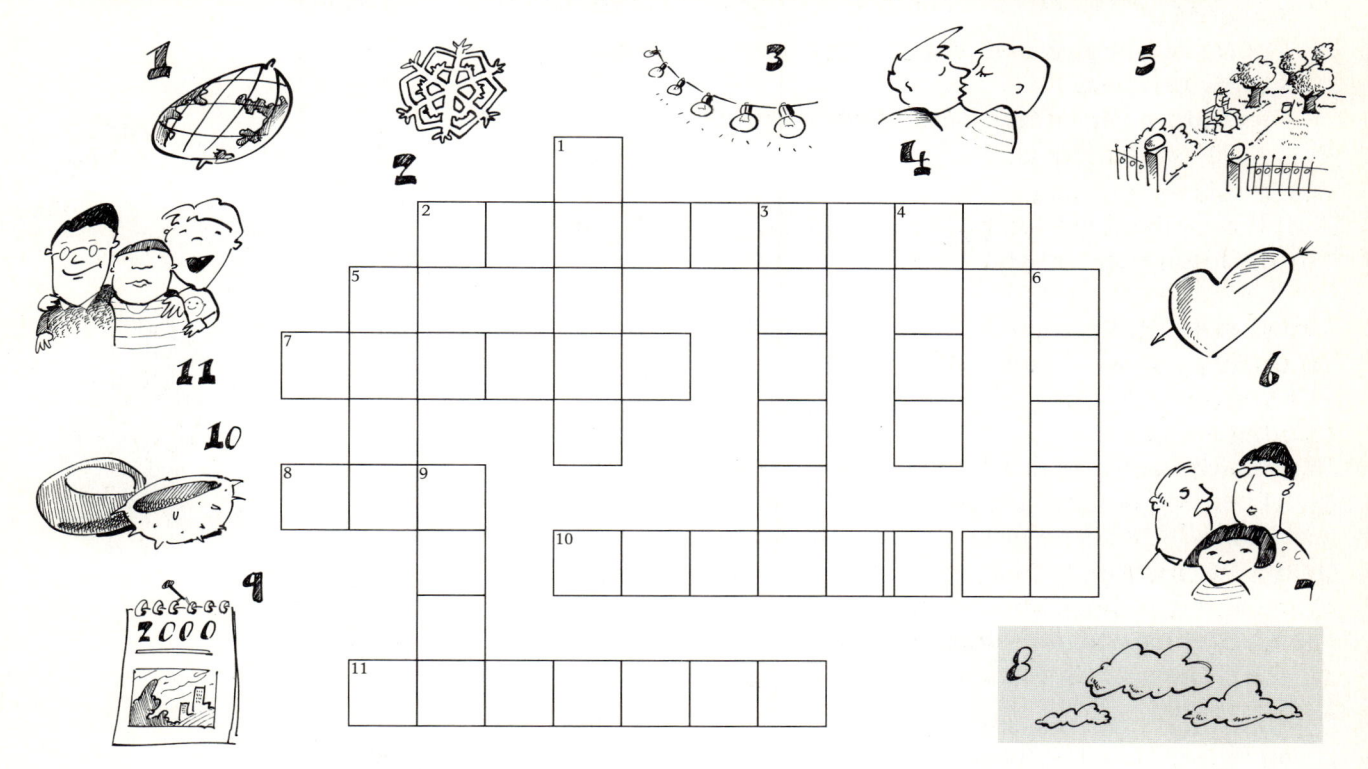

2. **Look at the pictures below and write in the names of these things.**

3. **It's Christmas morning and the stockings are full. Think of presents that could be in them, using the letters on the right.**

C _____
H _____
R _____
I _____
S _____
T _____
M _____
A _____
S _____

T _____
I _____
M _____
E _____

**4. Look at Carly's homepage about Christmas. Then design your own homepage.
You could:**
– write about yourself, your family, pets, hobbies…
– draw pictures.
– include a Christmas acrostic like Carly's.

Welcome to Carly's Homepage

I used to go to Welford and Wickham school but now I have moved on to secondary school. Thank you for visiting.

Hi, there,
My name is Carly. I am 10 years old and I have a pet called Blacky. She is a cat (I bet you can guess what colour she is). Yes, she is black. Do you like Christmas? I like it so much, I think the important thing about Christmas is giving and taking.

Here is an acrostic for you.

Christmas presents, some for me
Holly stuck on the tree,
Rip all the presents on this day,
Invitations on their way,
Singing all the Christmas carols,
The children playing in some barrels,
May we all come this way,
As for this very special day BECAUSE…
SANTA CLAUS IS ON HIS WAY!!!

Presents oh presents
Right under the tree,
Enough for you and enough for me!!
Some are big and some are tall
Endless presents look at them all!!
Nice big round ones and some quite flat
Tight and small ones, they mean more than that
So that's why presents are fun (in a way) and I can't wait until Christmas Day!

Now I am going to tell you about my brother. Well he has kind of hazel brown eyes and brown hair and a very squiggy nose and he has asthma. His best friends are Charlie, Shane, Tom, Barney, Michael, Jamie, and in the Juniors, Paul, George and James. And his best teachers are Miss Needles, Mrs Crisp and Mrs Pearce (as a supply teacher).

I think I will tell you about my hobbies now. Well I like writing, typing, drawing, watching *Home and Away* and then *Neighbours,* and best of all I like being friends with anybody! I'm sorry I didn't tell you much about myself at the beginning. It's just I am so excited about Christmas. Well I have brown hair (it's kind of long), brown eyes and I like eating!!!!
Well that will be all from me.

GOODBYE!